All One Era

STEPHEN CIPES

Stephen, Rie and Fortuna celebrating our "John and Yoko" wedding on the Spring Equinox 2010

Copyright © 2017 Stephen Cipes
alloneera.com

ISBN: 978-1-7751276-0-4

COVER CREDIT AND CERTIFICATION

Taken with a digital camera, the Summerhill Pyramid's energy is captured for all time.

Letter to Summerhill Pyramid Winery
Kelowna, BC

November 7, 2002

On Friday, October 18th 2001, I noticed that the harvest moon was visible before dark. It was beautiful. During a family diner, at the Summerhill Estate Winery bistro, conversation eventually turned to the gorgeous moon that evening. My niece suggested that I take a picture of the moon perched on top of the pyramid. After dinner, I went outside with my brother-in-law and I decided to take the picture.

The moon was so bright that I had to hide most of it behind the tip of the pyramid. I took the picture with my Minolta Dimage V11 5.2 mega pixel camera. You cannot imagine my surprise when I downloaded this image to my computer. I was stunned. I have never altered this picture file. I cannot explain it and have not had this happen on my other pictures, before or after.

I certify that this is the original image.

Laurie Giles
Certified Management Accountant
Port Coquitlam, British Columbia

This book contains special images called maxograms. When these images are viewed using the app from maxogram.com the images come alive right on the printed page and give you even more of the story!

To get started, just get the app from maxogram.com, open it, then use it to view any image bearing the icon above.

maxogram.com

CONTENTS

The time is NOW for love. We have arrived at perhaps the most pivotal point in our eternal journey. This era is highly conducive for us to return to our all-Knowing, all-receiving Grand Selves, with a capital S! We all have a truly Holy privilege of being able to let go and be Guided. This wondrous flow of loving energy longs to come through us freely once again. We are pure vessels for the messages of loving intention, and it behooves us to now establish gathering venues around the world that are highly conducive to the nourishing of our most lofty intentions. We are potentially an exalted population living in harmony with nature. This is our grand opportunity to merge with our living Earth and embrace our rich Oneness with Her.

ACKNOWLEDGMENTS

Thank you to my many friends and family members who have encouraged me to "Write a book Steve!" Their love for me, support and enthusiasm for my many stories about experiences demonstrating that "If I can actually create miracles, we all can!" I especially want to thank my wife Rie Oshita Cipes, our daughter Esther Ehisa (EE) Cipes, and my four great sons and their families for their patience and understanding for my very early morning writing, meditation and study that have sometimes stolen precious time from our joyous adventures.

I would like to acknowledge with love and deep gratitude, Joscelyn Duffy (joscelynduffy.com), author, collaborator, creative consultant and Reiki Master. I would also like to especially thank Matthew Jensen (jensenworks.com) for his soul-to-soul encouragement AND scholarly contributions. As well, I would like to give thanks to the many Masters, both modern day and historical, who have helped me to see so clearly the magnificence of us humans. As we proactively and joyously welcome our full dimensions, we catapult the prophesized Holy All One Era.

Stephen and Joscelyn Duffy at the dedication of a new Torah, commissioned in Israel, and donated by Stephen to Chabad Okanagan. This occasion marked the beginning of our working together on the All One Era manuscript.

Stephen presents a pre-release copy of All One Era to Anita Moorjani at a Kelowna reception, where she brought everyone to tears of joy presenting a magnificent link with those in other dimensions and her incredible encounter while on the "other side" with her father while she was in a coma. They forgave each other for unbearable expectations they had imposed on each other, which immediately set the pace for her complete, miraculous cancer remission! Anita's books have been translated internationally with sales in the millions of copies.

We deserve an awakening within our Selves that will bend every knee. From the soul of who I am, I call for a colossal surrender of our ego-based separation and a world-wide grassroots return to our ancient tribal gatherings with intentions of harmony with nature and ourselves on all levels.

FOREWORD

For many years, I worked as a personal assistant to Eckhart Tolle, bestselling author of The Power of Now. He inspired me to follow my journey of enlightenment by training in Thailand. It was there that I was bestowed the privilege of being the only Western woman granted a spiritual name by the revered Master Monk Prah Bhasakorn. As a Canadian living in Thailand, studying the Buddha's Dharma, I had a vision of a place called Kee Low Na. I had no idea what this place was like, but I was drawn to it.

After completing eight years, including one year of silent meditation, I was given a foundation of knowledge that would compel me forward into a new phase of my life. I knew, as I followed my heart, that I would bring my rich and blessed experiences to Kee Low Na, or Kelowna, British Columbia, Canada. The experience in my new home has been serene, as one glorious spirit after another joined my path, including the treasured encounter and presence of a man who is like a brother to me…or as he puts it, "You are da Momma and I am da Poppa." That man is Stephen Cipes.

It is an honor to write this foreword for my dear friend and spiritual colleague, Stephen. I immediately recognized his abilities as a leader and spiritual teacher from the very moment we met at a Summerhill Pyramid gathering, where he invited me to speak and offer blessings. Upon meeting, we understood in our hearts that we have a deep soulful connection for expanding love on this planet. Stephen continues to spark a wonderful light in my heart, reminiscent to that of my six years of close association with my former spiritual teacher, Eckhart Tolle.

Stephen Cipes is a visionary. He walks his talk of being "God in a body." As an entrepreneur, he welcomes thousands of visitors a day at his award-winning Summerhill Pyramid Winery, which he boasts is the most visited winery in Canada. All of his wines and the food at the bistro are organic and he is leading a vision to convert the entire Okanagan Valley to organic practices by the year 2020. More importantly, Stephen hosts new and full moon gatherings at the pyramid wine cellar, which he built to precision as a scale model of The Great Pyramid of Egypt. Following the pyramid meditations, he brings the community around the fire in a reproduction of an authentic Winter Kekuli –

an underground "pit house" that the Okanagan People dwelled in. Joining together in each other's Light, attendees unite for drumming and dancing. Having been a part of these gatherings, I have witnessed how Stephen is a natural host, opening his eighty-acre vineyard to "The Grand Teachings." He is living out his vision of bringing everyone back together, to nature, and to the roots of the All One Era message of unity.

His message is in harmony with many spiritual teachers and authors that I have had the privilege to work alongside. His writing is a masterful summation of the power and oneness alive in all of us. Stephen's book, All One Era, intertwines the Grand Teachings with stories from his own life experiences. It highlights an array of pivotal suggestions on how all of us can regain our own "God Power."

This book is a must-read for anyone ready to step into the authentic self of peace, clarity and serene confidence, or as Stephen puts it, welcome back the true power of our Genius Selves. It is for those wanting to return to nature, ceremony and community, and most importantly, return to the divinity they may have lost. This is a masterful read and epic tale told through Stephen's own accounts.

Stephen has written this book from his heart. In it, you will be witness to Stephen as he rises above his early childhood challenges of being on his own since age thirteen and becomes an entrepreneur with the world as his family. He takes us through an exciting and daring, yet playful synopsis of his many lives in this lifetime, with each shared memory catapulting the reader into what he calls "Fifth Dimensional Love."

I am delighted to wholeheartedly introduce Stephen's wondrous work, and I have highlighted a great number of his passages as ideal for individual workshop projects (a highlighted version is available at alloneera.com/workshops). He brings us an opportunity to establish a worldwide network with a return to unity and our power as the Grand All-Knowing Beings that he proclaims we are.

In loving Kindness, Maytawee
maytawee.ca

Stephen Cipes & former Thai Monk-Nun
Maytawee at Summerhill Pyramid Winery

7

"The All One Era:
Our Prophesized
Homecoming."

Stephen Cipes

INTRODUCTION

Dear Readers,

Not always, but often, I feel confident enough to speak from my heart, as God in a body. That is how I have tried to write this book. It is my highest dream that we all speak as God/Goddess in a body, and it is my hope that this book outlines a master plan for us all to reunite and celebrate our highest dreams and our original pure love intentions. I wish from my heart of hearts for everyone to join me as we rejoice in receiving the ever-present magnificence we bathe in called the Loving Universal Consciousness (LUC).

In the year 2000, I drafted an outline for a book with the title <u>My Trees, My Dolphins</u> while on a journey with Dr. Jose Cabanillas on his 600-acre medical research retreat in the Amazon jungle of Peru, where beautiful pink dolphins flourished in the fresh water. The primitive naked peoples living in huts along the river had decided to kill the dolphins, as these mammals had been eating the fish that was their sustenance. I also witnessed the trees being torn out by huge machines to make room for cows to graze for fast food restaurant chain hamburgers, and I watched the people line up to throw garbage over the bridge into the river, day and night. I cried out in horror, and became ill and disheartened. My cries, and all of our cries, are being heard now, at a time I pray is not too late.

We were all inspired by Kahlil Gibran's classic book, <u>The Prophet</u>: "A little while, a moment of rest upon the wind, and another woman shall bear me." The All One Era, the "Prophecy of Prophecies," is our ascension into the loving "no time". We are assimilating all of the dimensions by Knowingness…our Eternal Oneness. As an ascended human, our oneness is fully realized; as an ascended humanity, our Original Splendid Intention of unbounded love and of knowing our Selves, Nature and our Earth is renewed and flourishes. I have found that the key to our instant ascension is allowing Knowingness; the key to allowing Knowingness is surrender; the key to surrender is proactive receiving; the key to receiving is allowing Spirit to flow through us as conduits, as microcosms of the universe; AND the key to becoming a conduit is to proactively love life.

I wish to speak one-to-one, as an ambassador for the grandest platform we humans could ever embrace: our Knowingness of who we are. I speak to you as casually as a long-lost friend, an uncle, brother, or dad, a child of seven years of age in a body of a seasoned entrepreneur who has loved the world as his family since being on my own in the seventh grade, and a person who shares a life of extreme triumphs, abundance and total joy showing that we can all share in joy and abundance!

My life has felt like many lives in one. I have ventured down into the darkest places and lived among some of the most depressed people on earth. Since childhood, I have reached out to understand first-hand the truths and suffering of humanity, and the spaces in which we can welcome more peace, kindness and understanding with each other and with our precious Mother Earth. I have sought solace and enlightenment by embracing the traditions of nine different religions and I have felt oneness with those of all the ethnic backgrounds.

Born to Jewish parents, I grew up in an Irish-Italian neighborhood, and chose to become a devout Catholic for seven years, beginning in my late teens. I learned to cherish the work of Jesus and the Saints, instantly recognizing Jesus' teachings and saw that He was a pure vessel and conduit of Divine Spirit. That was the beginning of my quest to reveal that indeed we are all conduits of Spirit. For many years, I was deeply immersed in being Seventh Day Adventist and feel very blessed for having enjoyed that experience. I also drank in the teachings of Buddhism, Shintoism, Hinduism, Bahá'i, Judaism, and Taoism. To this day, I share each religion's teachings, while staying closely connected to the resounding messages of all of the Great Masters. Like my Native Aboriginal brothers and sisters, I reach out to the Earth Herself. In bare feet, we stand one-on-one with the stars, moon, and sun; we celebrate their cycles and become one. In sacred sweat lodges, we merge with the animals and the plants, and are even one with the rocks, the rivers, the sky, and the oceans. This is our true religion, and the golden thread that ties all religions and all of us together.

Through my life's journey, I have also been very blessed to learn from, work with, and become close to many beings of all ethnic backgrounds. In my heart of hearts, I am truly African American, Italian, Spanish, Russian, Japanese, Chinese, Egyptian, Native American, Greek, Irish, and German. My wish is for my life and the messages within these pages to transcend all religions, races, and business sectors, while at the same time being one with each of them. My yearning for deep understanding has taken me to a place where I truly feel like I am a composite of humanity, as we all are. We are all tribal. Every culture, religion, race, creed, and color began with gatherings around the fire. These roots unite us as they were and are our strength and soul memory. It takes a village to raise a child. It takes a return to our roots to recreate a heart-centered awakening and call to action.

We are taking back our power and lifting the veils of separation! We are opening our "receiving hearts" and welcoming our most basic universal soul memory! In nature-honoring gatherings, which are conducive to meditation, we are richly nourishing our natural ability to open our Selves, our "God Selves," to our infinite love, power and genius-level Knowingness.

In this era of highest vibration and unified conscious alignment, which officially began on December 21, 2012 – the ending of the ancient Mayan Calendar, we are welcoming the Master's return! The Master is us! Each of us is now catapulting our own ascension as we give our love to all there is and also open ourselves to receiving love!

The first model venue for All One Era gatherings has been established in Kelowna, British Columbia at Summerhill Pyramid Organic Winery. Since 1997, the season changes have been celebrated when the pyramid is most perfectly aligned and most effective, on the Solstices and Equinoxes. The Summerhill Pyramid[1], a sixty-foot square, four-story replica of The Great Pyramid of Egypt, serves as a cellar for all the organic wines produced and as a sacred chamber for meditations that are held in concert with the changes of nature. The Summer Solstice attracts record crowds to the pyramid every year. The Winter Solstice, with its traditional procession of guests

---

[1] See The Summerhill Pyramid at alloneera.com/pyramid

holding a candle and filing from the pyramid to the Makwala Memorial Kekuli always brings light on the darkest day of the year. The Spring and Fall Equinox gatherings have been joyous celebrations all these years, with dancing and drumming around the sacred fire in the Kekuli, alongside veggie potluck feasts. Since the Winter Solstice of December 21, 2012, the Kelowna community also celebrates the new moon every month in the pyramid for females only and men only in the Kekuli, and full moon for families in both the pyramid and Kekuli. With twenty-eight events a year, the community's contact list now numbers in the thousands of loyal enthusiasts and is growing every month.

Returning to gatherings is a gigantic step for humankind, conducive to catapulting ascension just by being in each other's bands of energy[2]!

This is my vision for humanity, to lift the veil with a specific proactive master plan of action, worldwide connections, and gatherings. We ARE God, Divine All One Forever Beings. This is the "Prophecy of Prophecies" and our original blessed eternal merger with Loving Universal Consciousness (LUC) – the loving cosmic vibrations that indeed we are, and perhaps our highest calling in the history of humanity. The most passionate and significant message that I am here to share is that we each have the magnificent power within us to affect our entire creation! We ARE God. We ARE Love. Everyone in their heart of hearts knows this most powerful of universal truths. The core foundation of this book is the revelation of the word "love". We humans are the conduits of the infinite cosmic consciousness that is yearning to be revealed as we both surrender and receive the LUC, that is us.

I wish to demonstrate that our greatest fear is the fear of our own grandness. We have the Divine Knowingness. In our stillness[3] as receivers and conduits of spirit, we Know all there is. There are none in our entire universe greater than we are, and none of us are greater than any other entities.

---

[2] See Valerie Hunt Video Showing Our Bands of Energy! alloneera.com/bioenergy

[3] See the Constance Kellough (Namaste Publishing) Innerbody Meditation website expanding on Eckhart Tolle's teachings: innerbodymeditation.com

We are all one, each a microcosm of the universe, and collectively the LUC. I am honored and humbled to be Guided and share the light of coming into our Knowingness, our genius state, where our bodies' electrical systems are in full vibratory resonance – a state we have all touched upon in dreams, meditations, and daydreams, and a state well worth proactively devoting our precious time in bodies to achieve.

At this time, I feel so "in service" and so privileged to now be actually setting forth guidelines and a working model for a worldwide network – a holistic way to joyfully and organically re-establish our Original Splendid Intention of ever-evolving consciousness and abundance, and our "quantum physics" of creating from moment-to-moment on our heavenly emerald planet. This book outlines the ultimate call to action. Fused within these pages is a focus on going within, where we are all one, in the glorious soul of the world. We have the ability to feel and Know the vibration of all of creation within our bodies. Through our mergence in such a space of awareness, we catapult a total rejuvenation, a colossal movement in love.

Our Divine Energy is now sweeping our planet rapidly, as we each take back our Holy power. We ARE Divine Beings whose time is NOW for love. The greatest service is to know our divinity.

With blessings, love, gratitude[4], and excitement for this wondrous new era,

Stephen - stephen@alloneera.com

---

[4] See alloneera.com/gratefulness

"Concerning matter, we have been all wrong.
What we have called matter is energy, whose vibration
has been so lowered as to be perceptible to the senses.
There is no matter."

Albert Einstein

"Heroic stories of Jesus, Buddha and history's masters, forged in the fire of singularity, have lead us here, now - Peering into the galactic abyss. Looking back for guidance we realize, finally and forever, that time has passed its relevance.

Understanding that the savior is us, we take our greatest leap. Inner and outer spaces merge, pulling us higher and closer, inside out.

The season calls for the thorn crown to blossom.
Kingdom has come, and the all one era is upon us."

Joshua Dawson
Genie, Dad, Lover of life.
iamgenie.org

"Within our microcosmic Selves, every healing and rejuvenating intention is Present."

Stephen Cipes

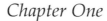

Chapter One

A VISION FOR HUMANITY

With all the many wondrous messages circulating in the world, there remains a huge void: **The return to our oneness.** I'd like to be openhearted and provide you with a stream of consciousness, so you might relate to why I feel so strongly about this.

It was exactly 3:18 a.m. on March 23, 2013, when I sat up and slipped into lotus position to behold the details of one of the most significant dreams of my life. I remember it well. I was in Osaka, Japan with my wife Rie and our daughter Esther. We were visiting Ojijan (Grandpa) and Obajan (Grandma) for the first time since Esther was born three years prior. We had just enjoyed seven glorious weeks touring the many beautiful shrines and temples of the country and were staying in a sixth-floor suite located in the heart of Osaka, near Kyoto. The setting and my vision in the dream were so real, so lucid, that I felt as though I was fully awake.

In the dream, I was standing alone, surveying far-reaching and deeply impacting worldly destruction and chaos. I stood simultaneously within entire cities cleared out by the worst storm in recorded history (which actually happened shortly thereafter in the Philippines) and within an enormous volcanic eruption that had just taken place in Iceland. I could see vast amounts of carbon spreading across the land; it was more carbon than our entire population could produce in hundreds of years (this also came to pass). I watched the shrinking of the ozone layer and disappearance of the condors (later confirmed by formal decree by The Hopi Elders). I observed with utter sadness the sharp rise of cancers in animals and humans following the devastating effects of constant spewing of radioactivity from the Fukushima nuclear power plant meltdown. I saw and felt devastation of plant life from vast amounts of radiation, and contamination of agriculture from the acid rain. I watched the bees and butterflies be the first species to deeply suffer the brutality of the huge chemical and biological altering of nature at the hands of greedy chemical farming companies. I stood at the heart of the Amazon rain forest, hearing the planet struggle to breathe as the greed of corporations tore down the trees to create soy bean and corn fields to feed cattle, whose gas depletes our ozone layer. I heard the cries of tortured whales, dolphins, elephants, and rare plants and animal species that were so rapidly becoming extinct, and I was aware of being so aghast by the physical impact of our complete absorption into the "human drama." The human drama, where we so often allow ourselves to be centered in fear and the perceived need for material and social status, rather than our lofty stewardship roles as co-creators.

As I witnessed the vividness of such travesty and destruction, from seemingly out of nowhere came an airplane, landing on a dime right before me. Emerging from the plane was a female person of glorious beauty. Her face was a composite of all the most magnificent female human faces I have ever had the privilege and honor of knowing, and her energy was one of indescribable total purity and love. This radiant entity proceeded to reach out her hand and so lovingly touch the land before me, gifting visible magical healing energy upon every being, every circumstance, every plant and every animal. I got a glimpse of her unlimited love, and in that moment, it transformed the entire meaning of the word love. I'm unable to fathom, much less articulate, just what she did, who she touched, or how she did it, but what she did was all-encompassing and all-Divine – a total and complete rejuvenation of everything back to teeming life! At the same time, I was shocked to behold her hand shriveling as she swept it across the earth. I reached out to help her, but she signaled me a loving gesture that her hand was a small sacrifice for such a gain. She then leaned forward and told me not to worry, as there would surely be a way to reform her hand later. We enjoyed a loving, reassuring embrace and acknowledgement that indeed everything in the world is wondrous and perfect in every way. She hopped back on her little plane and took off, without a runway or rolling start. She simply disappeared as quickly as she had appeared, leaving me awestruck.

For the two hours that followed the dream, I slipped into lotus position and sat in deep meditation. During my reflection, I felt an overwhelming feeling of blessedness to have seen the actual face of God/Goddess and to have been with this Holy Composite Being who emanated such love that *She* gave her hand to heal the world, while radiantly shining with love so deep there wasn't a trace of concern about her own wellbeing. She had gestured to me that her hand is extended out for all time!

As I stood in her presence in the dream, I felt as though I was one with God like never before. She graces us and is one in eternal unconditional love. The profound lesson here is that there is no distinction between us, we too are one in eternal unconditional love. She came to me to show all of us that we can perform miracles! The Diva from the skies left an everlasting impression on my soul. I knew I had been blessed with the rarest of honors. I had beheld the angelic face of glorious, pure, cosmic love.

The Osaka dream, while being one of the most profound, is only one in a series of constant lucid dreams that I've had since childhood. In my dreams, I "travel" to ancient times and ancient places and to "future places," where we are in "domes" traveling in space. Frequently, I have dreams where I can fly, and actually find myself working hard to move my wings. I am in awe of being in a body. It is a glorious opportunity, but also a great challenge and burden, as we are "trapped" by the lowered frequencies required to be materialized. However, perhaps our having these bodies is our grandest opportunity to feel, know and nourish our Forever Souls with the enrichment of ever-expanding consciousness, love and compassion. Through the clarity of our dreams and visions, we are connected to energy and awareness that is multi-dimensional, and as we merge ourselves proactively with all dimensions, we have the opportunity to become conduits of pure love in bodies.

Chief Gary Oker has served for many years as "the Chief of the Chiefs" of the Northwestern Nations in Canada. In the tradition of the original peoples, songs and drumming around the fire come from visions and dreams, and are inspired by the Grandmothers and Grandfathers, the ancestors who speak to us through the fire. After reading this manuscript, Chief Oker supported me by saying, "Dreamers' songs, are found by retuning it from dreamland to physical time to understand. I believe I understand what you mean as "be in one". **It is when you find your power song to heal people.**"

The images of desolation and catastrophes within my dream were a paralleled reflection of our sad realities. Our world has never been so close to complete and utter destruction. The earth has been weakened by the punches she has received at our hands; and what she may have survived in past decades, she cannot anymore. She is struggling, crying out for us to be in total consciousness with her to achieve harmony. As we begin to gather and share our closeness with our Earth, we bring in the light. As we all know, a single candle can light the darkest room. We are living on borrowed time. The pleas of starving children and cries of dying whales and elephants are the Earth letting out her last sighs of wanting to die. We have tortured her so, living from a space within ourselves that has not been aligned with *Godance* (Guidance as one with God), or Divine Guidance.

The state of the planet today is much more seriously in jeopardy than we have been willing to accept as a whole, giving us all a very critical purpose in this lifetime. Today, Al Gore's *An Inconvenient Truth* (2006) and Leonardo DiCaprio's beautiful new movie, *Before the Flood* (2016), clearly demonstrate how we humans live our daily lives on levels of "taking" that are far beyond our planet's ability to catch up.

What would it take to have a wake-up call of major proportions? Have we gone too far beyond the tipping point to respond and to contribute, even if we were Guided from the highest sources? Will it take another war to wake us up? A gripping global economic collapse? A tidal wave that sets off nuclear reactors and poisons us all with cancerous radiation? How about the melting of our ice and the rising of the sea, flooding land where over forty percent of our population resides? How about another ice age, as predicted? Why did *An Inconvenient Truth* not have an impact? It was there for all to see, and what did the world do? They held world summits and committed to lowering the carbon footprint using economic sanctions. And did they lower it? No! It was a joke. Dr. David Suzuki pointed out that the politicians who voted to lower it are no longer in office and those who are now are not obligated to adhere to those commitments. He also pointed out that taxing industry with heavy fines, if they keep up spewing and polluting, is a joke. They just pass the costs along to the consumers. There is no way to enforce these noble but weak intentions.

As we are finally now sadly realizing, we are living in a world that has become entirely affected by our greedy materialism and its resultant pollution. Everyone is literally being drained by huge amounts of toxins in our foods that we've never had before. The whales and the dolphins have been severely affected by sonar emitted by military forces; the fish are getting cancer from spewing radiation and are full of mercury; every ecosystem is absorbing pharmaceuticals; and our precious original seeds, plants, animals and many aboriginal humans are rapidly becoming extinct…all notwithstanding the valid argument that indeed one eruption by a volcano may emit more carbon than all of our factories put together. **We now know that we are intrinsically connected to that eruption and to all of nature. We can demonstrate that we have the power to actually affect nature! We have a Holy calling – a time in these extraordinary times, to re-enter our Oneness, our glory of taking back our power! We no longer have the luxury of throwing our hands in the air and giving away our power. Carpe Diem, seize the NOW. We are now rising to the occasion!**

There is now the greatest urgency for self-sufficiency and self-rejuvenation. Never before has there been a more urgent, planet-wide need to grow our own food, to drink only clean water, breathe clean air, and minimize our exposure to the far-reaching pollution. **The most urgent need we currently have, for all of us beings, is for our fragile bodies (our temples) to return to their highly in-tune, harmonic vibration.** On the brink of unprecedented planet-wide deterioration, we are realizing that only by going within do we stand a real chance to return to our oneness with nature and begin the physical restoration of our Earth and of our Selves. It is a pivotal point, where we become proactive in releasing and surrendering our natural ego (that all in body have), and acknowledge the blessing of our original nature: Feminine Receiving, conducive to receiving Guidance and instantly becoming Conduits of Spirit once again! As conduits, our bodies become our tools to create; and we, as the collective Holy Creators, ascend to being as one with all there is!

A wonderfully worthy passage to this effect is found in chapter 2 of *The Hermetica: The Lost Wisdom of the Pharaohs,* a revival of the ancient Emerald Tablets by Timothy Freke and Peter Gandy:

➤ Hermes derives his wisdom from a dramatic mystical revelation. While his mind is alert, yet still and empty, he hears God speaking to him. Hermes asks to be shown the true nature of reality, and suddenly everything begins to change before him.

➤ In a mysterious vision, he witnesses the creation of the world. This vision is not meant to be understood intellectually, but contemplated like images from dreams. However, we can explore a little of its deep meaning.

➤ Hermes' first experience is of an all-embracing Divine Light, which as he watches casts a shadow like dark restless water. Later he is told that this Light is the Mind of God, and the dark waters are the unlimited potential out of which God will fashion the universe.

➤ This is a mystical vision of the first act of creation, remarkably similar to the modern scientific theory of the Big Bang. An explosion of light and energy slowly cools to become the black womb of space, into which suns and planets and finally ourselves are born.

➤ This birth, like any birth, is accompanied by pain, and Hermes hears an inarticulate cry of suffering from the turbulent depths. The Light then speaks a Word which calms the chaotic waters.

➤ This Word is like a blueprint that will organize a structured cosmos out of the chaos. Modern science might call it the fundamental Laws of Nature. This Word is the first idea in the Mind of God, from which everything springs.

➤ Initiated into the secrets of the creation Hermes receives his Divine mission from the Supreme Being. Only this Knowledge he is told can save those who live in darkness. Hermes must become a spiritual guide to all Mankind.

As we ascend in our Knowingness and gather and re-harmonize with our earth, we come into the revelation that we are one with Divinity. I'd like to coin the word "Knowingness" with a capital "K" throughout these messages. Knowingness is a word that has no element of doubt and aptly describes our ability to be conduits of the cosmic and natural vibrations that surround each of us and all there is at all times. It is that magical, wispy, silent yet loud, transparent yet color-filled, welling feeling of joy that titillates every atom of every cell in our bodies, flooding in as we surrender and **let go and let God**, instead of holding on to our EGO (Edging God Out) selves focusing on wanting. As we open, we receive and merge with the "I Am" Holy Presence, where we are one with, feeling and knowing the Guidance, or the revelation that we are all Guided, versus us egotistically gloating over our achievements or being disappointed in our failures. Guidance is the subtle Knowingness that is sometimes seen only in later reflection.

Our Knowingness can be enhanced greatly as we align our lives with love, gratitude and a return to an organic nature. The honoring of ourselves and of our intimate connection with all of nature and our entire universe leads us to being in tune with our Original Splendid Intention, where we set forth a vision of an ever-expanding Holy loving energy, both physically and spiritually. We can embrace Holiness – the swirling mass of loving energy that makes up the ethereal plane of consciousness – and welcome it into our everyday lives. While all of these things may sound heady, they actually come to us in a flash as soon as we open our feminine receiving channels and begin to behold the flow of loving energy known as Loving Universal Consciousness (LUC), a collection of our mutual clarity and highest vibration at all times. As givers and receivers, we ARE the LUC. It is discovered when we go within to our hearts, our dreams, our soul memories, our essence, and our Knowingness. We can term it intuition, consciousness, Higher Self, or any term that is comfortable. To proactively acknowledge this constant swirling energy is to behold our own Eternal Grandness and more importantly, our Presence in these precious bodies.

Consciousness is our gift. We have the unique opportunity in this blessed new era to all go within to open and surrender to Spirit. The time is now for love. The time is now for us all to start gathering regularly, as we have for eons, honoring nature and opening and surrendering to the luminous love that surrounds us, replenishing our super-consciousness. The time is now to return to our hearts. This is the only way we will have a chance to save our splendid creation, our precious playground, our sacred sublime home. We created Earth, where we enjoy the ideal conditions to prosper and flourish in abundance and peace and joy in ingenious bodies that are, each and every one, a microcosm of the entire universe. Selah!

~

*"The environmental movement
has failed. We've won some pyrrhic
battles, but we lost the war
because we failed to change
consciousness surrounding these issues. "*

Environmental Activist Dr. David Suzuki summarizes our current situation
in his personal quote for this book.

Many moons later, I found myself in a continuation of the Osaka dream, but without the honor of gazing upon the composite luminous face of the Goddess whose hand shriveled as She cleansed the earth before my eyes. In this new dream, it was only me, standing as one, amidst the chaos, crisis, destruction, fear, and despair that surrounded me. I stood as the collective of all of us. I was facing the momentous burden of repairing the damage we have done to our Earth, and to ourselves. I felt within me a holistic connectedness with our Earth, and instantly knew and felt our grandness and oneness, and how all-powerful this golden connection was and is key to our saving our precious Earth. It was a jolt of empathy, understanding, contemplation, compassion, forgiveness and unconditional love for myself and all there is.

In this dream, I began to dive deeper into the truths of our world. As I wove through countries in crisis and fear-driven wars, I found myself landing on a filth-ridden street in an industrial section of an Asian city. The air was laden with pollution and heavy tobacco smoke. There, I came across a baby elephant lying helplessly before me. Gray and almost lifeless, he cried out for help to save his species and his home. Calling out into the streets, I attempted to echo the elephant's cries for help. Sadly, all of those who passed before me seemed lost, submerged in a sea of arguments, heated ego-based controversy, and the hot pursuit of material goods. They acted so far removed and detached from the truths that the dying baby elephant represented. Within me welled the stinging perspective of how the majority of all of our lives have become a living travesty and tragedy.

I was dying too, and all I could do was open my heart and just be with the elephant. As I stood there, one with my dying friend, a gust of wind brushed before us and swept a crumpled piece of paper before my feet. Bending to my knees, I picked it up and smoothed it out. It was a sheet torn from scriptures, the very last paragraph of the Hebrew Torah, The Five Books of Moses.

Malachi (3: 22, 23, and 24): *Remember ye the Law of Moses My servant, Which I commanded unto him in Horeb for all Israel, Even statutes and ordinances. Behold, I will send you Elijah the prophet before the coming of the great and terrible day of the Lord. And he shall turn the heart of the fathers to the children, and the heart of the children to their fathers; Lest I come and smite the land with utter destruction.*

In that moment, I saw we collectively *ARE* Elijah the Prophet. This is our one heart that we all know and love! I saw clearly that to turn our hearts is to surrender our ego selves and reunite as one. That was precisely how I felt with that baby elephant. I wanted to do everything possible to give him new life. It was a tie so strong I was willing to die for him. Few of us have been willing to die for each other. This is the time of being in the universal wave, when a sentiment this strong comes to each of us, and is captured in the name of love and in our return to our glory.

Awakening from this dream that took me into the depths of despair and strife, I was overcome by a calling for all of us to save our Earth and ourselves. We have numbed and lowered our vibration levels to a point where we are barely able to receive, much less be proactively one with the forever streaming Loving Universal Consciousness (LUC). Is it due to the toxins and pollutants that now permeate our planet? Is it due to our addiction to radiation-emitting electronic screens, or to our processed chemical foods, drugs and alcohol? Is it the extreme emotional drain of the fascination with "the human drama", our attachment to three-dimensional existence? Much like the Goddess in my Osaka dream, I would gladly sacrifice my hand and even my life. Could we now collectively wave our hands and correct all of this?

To mitigate the looming (Malachai) prophesized "utter destruction" of our planet (in the form of a pole reversal, ice age, plague or nuclear disaster), we have a Divine Calling to return to our power as

Grand Beings. **We deserve an awakening within our Selves that will bend every knee. From the soul of who I am, (where there has always existed a kinship with not only the baby elephant in my dream, but all animals and all the beloved plants and all of humanity), I call for a colossal surrender of our ego-based separation and a world-wide grassroots return to our ancient tribal gatherings with intentions of harmony with nature and ourselves on all levels.**

We *Know* in our heart of hearts that it is not too late. Even though we have progressed so close to the brink of utter destruction, we *Know* it is not too late to shift our world back to its natural glorious statement; it is a truth felt deeply in our souls. It is a call for a mighty new global movement.

All we need to do is allow the surrender of our egos and opening of our X chromosomes – our feminine receiving heart Selves – simply BE conduits of Spirit. BE God! This is achieved when we quiet ourselves completely, with patience and focus on the breath. By focusing on the breath, we eliminate the constant chatter of the mind and allow the ever-constant Loving Universal Consciousness to come through our hearts.

Acknowledging the well-accepted premise that all of our emotions evolve from the basis of either fear or love is an important step toward our ascension into multi-dimensions. You will Know when you are Guided. In spite of being the most advanced technical civilization in our recorded history, we are presently in one of the darkest times in all of history. Never have there been so many millions of lost souls, and so many tyrants, so much greed, want, and destruction, and flagrant ignorance of our Divine Unity, or of our dormant all-Knowingness.

As we rise above the three-dimensional human plane, ruled by fear, ego, and materialism; we enter into the dimensions of love, forgiveness, and Divine inspiration…and Godance. As we bridge what we realize, when in those higher vibrating dimensions, into our human lives, we begin to co-create the holiest of planes. Jesus, Moses, Buddha, Gandhi, and all of the great Prophets were models who did just this, because they were one with all there is. We each need to reclaim our power and brightly shine, each and every one of us, because we too are models.

Just for a day, dismiss any and all thoughts about anything material, even of food and drink.

Just for a day, dismiss any thoughts about relationships.

Just for a day, release any thoughts about our status.

Just for a day, release talking and be silent.

Just for a day, walk for a long time with your eyes down, your chest out, stomach in, shoulders back, wearing an inner smile.

Just for a day, let all discomforts go and be oblivious to cold, heat, hunger, thirst, itchiness and yearnings. Have no wants and just BE...content.

Just for a moment, let go of all inhibitions and CHANT! Feel the chant in every part of your body. Let it come from every muscle, every atom of every cell, and let it rock you, as an observer.

Just for a day, KNOW your KNOWINGNESS. Hear your thoughts, feel them, be them, behold your Self as a being in onement with all there is!

Just for a day, let go of ambitions, goals, hopes and all cares, allowing our feminine receiving Selves to be conduits of spirit, welcoming Guidance as we create from moment to moment. As creators or THE Creator (as All One Forever Beings), envision your energy as expanding with LOVE in every nanosecond AND by proactively spreading that LOVE!

Dr. David Suzuki is an award-winning scientist, environmentalist and broadcaster, and the founder of the Blue Dot movement in recognition of every Canadian's right to live in a healthy environment. Here, he and Stephen Cipes meet at a Water Conference in Kelowna, British Columbia, Canada on October 14, 2015, as they discuss the natural alignment of the Blue Dot movement and the All One Era. The day was synergistic, as Dr. Suzuki, along with Mayors and Chiefs in attendance, sign the DECLARATION to convert the Okanagan Valley back to original pristineness by transitioning all lawns, farms, schools and municipal areas to certified organic practices by the year 2020 – the Organic Okanagan 2020 Vision (sign the DECLARATION at organicokanagan.com).

*"Do not take this changing picture
of life and death seriously.
Behold your immortality!
It is the most joyous
realization you can experience."*

Paramahansa Yogananda,
Autobiography of a Yogi

Chapter Two

THE ALL ONE ERA

Prior to December 21, 2012, we lived in an aggressive era based on the interpretations of the bible that man is here to dominate the earth…when in fact, we are here to be one with the earth. However, the period leading up to the All One Era is a triumph for humanity in many ways. We made huge strides in relieving our burdens of physical work with vast technological and industrial advances; though it has also been an era focused on masculine domination, and the aftermath of all that we've created follows us. In such a very short time, we have created the monster of the heartless corporate machine with the bottom line as its sole purpose, and we are giving away our power to government leaders with similar mandates. The eight billion of us now not only have in place a way of living that far exceeds our planet's ability to recover, but we also have in our keeping the technological and militant means of annihilating all life. We have been driven by our constant co-venture in creation to build a "better lifestyle" for humanity – a noble and grand intention, but now, in this new era, we clearly see that the price for all this technology, combined with our warfare sophistication, puts us on the precipice of utter destruction. Left to escalate in the hands of monsters, it is only a matter of how long it will take.

The ancient chart carved into a rock wall by the Hopi Elders shows a crossroads that divides around the date of December 21, 2012, which is the exact date that the ancient Mayan moon calendar ends. Interestingly, this date was prophesized eons ago by many separate groups of peoples to be the beginning of a new era. It is the time when the elders of the Mayan, Hopi, and many Aboriginal civilizations predicted there to be a choice for us to make. The choice is simple yet profound. Are we to continue the line on the rock upwards toward certain destruction and demise with our greedy, selfish, material, and aggressive quests, or are we to now return to our Splendid Intention, our original glory? Humanity can continue with its egotistical ways or our souls can come back together in oneness with all.

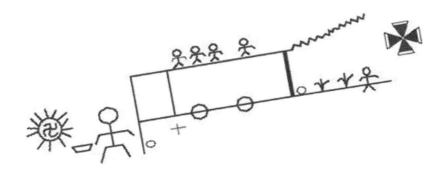

Diagram of the etching from the Prophecy Stone.
(See photo of the Hopi Prophecy stone at the end of the chapter.)

While living in the countryside of Bedford, New York in 1982, I had a very clear vision of us all being one. At that time, there had been a cold war brewing viciously between Russia and the United States, as well as extreme unrest in most of the world. We all felt us being on the brink of World War III. Fueled by a quest to bring humanity to its senses, I was Guided to dive deeper into the study of the Grand Teachings. I found the first of the Ten Commandments in the Hebrew Bible: *Exodus 20: So Moses went down unto the people, and told them. 1"And God spoke all these words saying: 2"I am the Lord thy God, who brought you out of the land of Egypt, out of the house of bondage. 3"Thou shalt have no other gods before Me.* I immediately remembered having pondered that commandment at my Bar Mitzvah in 1957, where it bothered me to give my power away to a fear-based God outside of myself! I was too young then…but in 1982, I had an ah-ha moment! What if Moses' words literally were meant to instill that indeed "*I* am the Lord your God…you will have no other Gods before me." Later on, we talk about Moses' plight, where he knew he was a total Conduit of Spirit and had the task of bringing the message to his people. The energy rose within me so greatly that I sat in silent meditation all day and night and proclaimed to myself that *From the Lord God of my being unto the Lord God of all beings on earth, we are One! We ARE God. We shall have no other Gods before Us.* We need to take back our power and BE God to be instantly Guided; and if we don't, we are lost souls sleeping in the dust, awaiting ascension.

Since that time, it is obvious to me, with so many earth changes, and the disappearance of the condors and the ozone layer, that we can no longer afford to throw our hands in the air, giving away our precious Holy power. Our intentions are all-powerful. We have the collective essence to merge with and Guide Nature! From ancient times, perhaps since the beginning of creation, we have carried both the burdens of enormous disappointment and the joy of the grandest of triumphs, with life itself being the most triumphant.

The blueprint for the All One Era is revealed constantly. During one occasion, my dog Wolf Girl and I had hiked to the top of the mountain and looked down upon the eighty-four-mile long Okanagan lake. As we stood there beholding the magnificence of the wondrous valley, it was clear to me that the essence of who we are is not solely in the beauty of the place where we live (the planet, the universe, the stars), the real beauty is in our Forever Souls, our hearts and eternal Selves. In moments and locales where the world around us showcases deterioration spurred by industrialization and pollution, or faces utter destruction, we know that the strength to reinvigorate the planet lies within us. We know that when in our power, we can no longer tolerate further human-made depletion. Our power is much stronger and farther reaching than we have ever taken credit for. It is this grand awakening that exonerates us from the present catastrophic ignorance and apathy leading us into oblivion.

The prophecy of the All One Era is that we know in our heart of hearts that we ARE God, the original creators of the universe, all-Knowing and all One. To come into our own Selves is to know our real power and the energy that can change the climate, our world and everything about us. This Knowingness is undeniable, because this IS who we are. There is no separation between us and the creation of matter, which simply is materialization of slower vibration of energy. Energy is love, the glue of the universe, love of our own grandness and all there is…better known as Glorious Oneness.

While the name of God is Holy, and all names for God are Holy, we have come to an awakening that indeed God and all that this Holy name carries is as dust without us, just as we are as dust without the realization of our oneness with God. The essence of this Prophecy of Prophecies lies deep in our soul memories. In the Hebrew bible, this is the response God gave when Moses asked him his name: Exodus 3:14: "And God said unto Moses, I am HE WHO IS."

The All One Era is our prophesized homecoming – our deserved release of all fear-based chaos, aggression, misery and guilt. We are All One, as Divine Eternal Beings, in bodies on our splendid creation with our precious animals, plants, earth, water, air sun, moon and stars – one ever-expanding alive, flourishing, love-based multidimensional consciousness that encompasses all that is, all that has been and all there shall ever be. By nourishing all life, and by choosing alive nutrition and an alive lifestyle to strengthen the silver cord between us as spirits in bodies and simultaneously as spirits in <u>The Holy Eternal Celestial Council</u> – the center of all of life and all of consciousness – we refresh our soul memory of who we are…we are <u>All One Forever Beings</u>.

Nature and the environment have always impassioned me. My instinct has always been to be one with the earth, touching it with my bare hands and feet. As a child, my time was spent playing in the dirt and climbing trees. Throughout my life, I was blessed with splendid collaborations with nature, and many firsts. One of the first vivid life-changing experiences was when I read the book *Bridey Murphy* in the sixth grade. Bridey was an American housewife who had been hypnotized and brought back to her earliest childhood and then further regressed into her past life, which had taken place in the 1700s in Ireland. She began speaking in her original Irish brogue, describing all the personal and factual things she experienced while in her life in Ireland. The book details how many of these actual places and things were later verified. This opened my soul memory of my personal past lives, and the realization that we are eternal beings. Today, the book *Many Lives, Many Masters* by Brian Weiss, MD tells the true story of a prominent psychiatrist, his young patient and the past-life therapy that changed both of their lives. Being All One Forever Beings AND being individuals in bodies is a brilliant and thrilling combination, filling our lives with Grand Purpose on a magnificent plane.

Having always known and embraced my purpose to BE a microcosm of the macrocosm, and the Grandest version of Stephen Cipes that I could be, I have consciously encouraged myself to proactively BE God in a body in this, my life. My plans to build have always been endless, with a boundless flow of ideas, which I then, with Guidance, and a sharing of my visions, manifest. As a land broker and developer in the Westchester suburbs of New York City in the early 1960s, I spearheaded cluster zoning to protect wetlands and steep slopes at a time when there were hardly any environmental protection laws. I was also crusading for the well-being of our planet as one of the founders of The Environmental Movement. My fellow long-haired hippies and I vehemently protested the burning of number six fuel and coal for heating in my highly-polluted native New York City. Simultaneously, we actually developed one of the first models of recycling and spread the wisdoms of re-usage. In spite of our encouraging progress, the gallant recycling efforts, and great strides we made in cleaning our air, the state of our Earth continued to deteriorate at alarming rates in the five decades that followed, and sadly toxic level pollution has now penetrated and permeated all of the planet and all living creatures, including us! (Astonishingly, there is evidence of toxins even in newborn babies.)

As the founder of Summerhill Pyramid Organic Winery in British Columbia, I built a "model of man and nature" and I am realizing my vision of being a conduit for heart-centered business. Business success is a platform from which we can be heard and hear on many levels. It enables us to live out Master Jesus' grand teaching: "The greatest gift is to give of one's self". I live with genuine daily excitement to give to the world, in great part by using business as a platform to share spiritual awareness. If I were to define entrepreneurship, I would say, "an entrepreneur is the highest profession. It is one who surrounds themselves with the Knowingness to manifest their vision." Building and operating "the most visited winery in Canada," as an organic winery and bistro, and as a model of harmony with nature and of giving back to nature, is a thrill and an honor. The opportunity to co-create with nature and actually demonstrate being a microcosm of the macrocosm from moment to moment delivers a highly-satisfying sense of accomplishment and of furthest-reaching universal significance. More importantly, it is a model of how each of us is as abundant as life itself!

From very early on in life, I knew my soul purpose. Something bigger cried out from within me, asking me to go forth and bring others together with me so that we may expand together, and be of full assistance in the realization of each other's highest aspirations. There was and is an undeniable tie between acknowledging the divinity in others and respecting others and our planet. Perhaps it was my childhood environment of constant tension between my parents and their bloody fight that set me completely alone in this world in 1957 at age thirteen… I always knew that there is no such thing as being completely alone. Having that solace along with creating a solid platform as an entrepreneur, I'm honored to say that I've fully allowed myself to be Guided. I've been an instrument, as we can all be instruments in how things in this world are. I have been, and continue to demonstrate being a conduit for love, peace, respect, and profound conscious awakening. Most importantly, I've acknowledged my purpose as a conduit of Spirit.

~

Honoring Our Holy Grand Purpose

~

Consciously or unconsciously, we are all aligned with our purpose – one we decided upon well before choosing to be born or re-born. The earlier we gain clarity of our purpose, the better, so we may nurture it and watch it unfold before us. I have learned that we should follow the energy and not the issue. Among the many revelations being brought forth in this new era is the alignment with our "Original Splendid Purpose," individually and collectively. We are finding that our real soul purpose has little or nothing to do with our business, religious, political, ethnic backgrounds or pursuits. Our grandest purpose is our contribution to the whole. It is the foundation upon which our own personal evolvement takes place! Sometimes it takes a lifetime to know our original purpose, and sometimes we are blessed to find it out at an early age. In my life, I've always felt a constant calling. A reading with Oracle Judith K. Moore and Dr. Sean Sands on July 19, 2014 greatly strengthened my confidence.[5]

---

[5] To learn more about Judith K. Moore's work as an oracle and as the author of *Crop Circles Revealed*, see alloneera.com/recordsofcreation.

Judith: *And then it said that the light will flow through the Staff of Moses into you, to illuminate God's Holy Presence.*[6]

Stephen: *Um, great.*

Judith*: And it spoke of the fulfillment of prophecies and the Enochian gospels, and it said that the Book of the Law of One is the Twelfth Enochian Gospel. So, I will be able to transfer this to you when we finish today.*

Stephen: *Wonderful!*

Judith: *But it's the basic information, and I'm recording* now.

Stephen: *Okay.*

Judith*: It said that the fulfillment of prophecy is not about the translation of prophecy. It is about the power of prophecy, and that when the Ark of the Covenant came to the Earth, there were archives of the Ark of the Covenant, and they brought a force, a God force to connect to the consciousness of humanity. The archives, once opened in the Ark of the Covenant, moved a force for humanity that had to fulfill the covenant by fulfilling the prophecies of light; that now at this time of all times, all prophecies must become one prophecy, and it is the prophecy of the Law of One. And seek not the interpretations of prophets or prophecy, but to know that each of them had to fulfill the covenant that was brought by the Ark and spelled out for humanity in the archives of light, the archives of the Ark of the Covenant. You have a line, Stephen, that goes back to the bloodlines of the prophets.*

Stephen: *I feel it very strongly, Judith. It has been motivating me all of my life.*

---

[6] The energetic properties of The Staff of Moses and The Ark of the Covenant are defined in detail in chapter 32 ("Ptahhotep's Instruction: The Seven Octaves of Vibration and The Ark of the Covenant") of *Initiation* by Elisabeth Haich.

Judith: *And you are one of the Covenant, and that means that your destiny is to fulfill the prophecies of light because they said that when all prophecies become one prophecy in the energy, in the force of the God Source on Earth, that then the Book of the Law of One shall be opened, and the opening of the Book of the Law of One fulfills the prophecy of the movement of liberation, and the force of Moses is a force of liberation. Humanity escaped enslavement but wandered alone in the desert lost and disconnected from the manna.*

Stephen: *Yes.*

Judith: *And then found the Source, was brought to the Heavenly Source, and that is the movement...from bondage to liberation to being lost souls, to the opening of the Book of the Law of One opens the gateways to the heavenly and Earthly kingdoms.*

Stephen: *Yes.*

Judith*: That bring the children home, and you have much to do with this because when the light of the Ark of the Covenant flows through the Staff of Moses and fills you with the power of the God Source, it opens, it opens the light, the light of the Book of One, the Law of One, that all children of God, which are all children of all humanity, will live then by the power of the Law of One in the Covenant of Light that fulfills the Prophecy of Revelations. Very few people know you; very few people are allowed to see you and you do not always see yourself. There is an image behind an image. There is a power behind anything that is of the Earthly realm. That is the power of prophecy embodied through your blood line because you have stood on destiny lines and appeared in the human form to be a witness of prophecy along a time line that was put in motion by the forces of Creation manifest[ed] through the power of the Living Ark, and thus as one of the brethren of the Ark of the Covenant, you were one of the Masters of Light who received the Ark when it descended from the Heavenly realm, and it was visible to you then. You have traveled with it; you have traveled with the Ark.*

Stephen: *Yes, at home.*

Judith: *A lot of energy is coming in, Stephen. Humanity has been lost to itself and the Divine nature of the God Source. The power of the Revelations of the Twelfth Book of Enoch opens a covenant of light, which forms; it forms the power that moves the destiny of human history. You are to feel now the power that moves the destiny of human history.*
Stephen: *Yes.*

Judith: *It cannot be in the hands of magistrates or god kings.*

Stephen: *No.*

Judith: *It must be in the hearts of those who serve selflessly and have walked through time, as you have, have witnessed the prophecies, have heard the words of the prophets and have carried the staff, the staff of the Mosaic order. This promise of liberation is beyond comprehension.*

Stephen: *Yes.*

Judith: *It is the power of light that seals all realms of darkness and brings forth into the sight, into the sight of humanity that which illuminates Divine Oneness, and you will continue to follow this path of prophecy, the path of divination of the Holy Source of God's Presence; through the prophets and through the Covenant, you will be compelled to continue to follow it, for it is the compelling force of your Soul, and you know this. Until at last you reach the doorway of light of the Thirteenth Temple, for there are Twelve Temples in the House of Light, in the House of Light of your— in the House of Moses, there are 12 Temples in the House of Moses, there are 12 Temples. You have built a temple there. It is the Twelfth Temple. It opens the way to the doorway of light to the Thirteenth Temple.*

Stephen: *Yes.*

Judith: *Your life has been — your lives have been a sacred journey of the kabalistic formulas, for you have walked a pattern with your lives, with the kabalistic masters.*

Stephen: *Yes.*

Judith: *That reveals the power of one, and no Earthly force can resist this Covenant of Light. There are those who speak of secret societies, and this is minor compared to the power of this mystical order of light that is unseen, and it is only connected through super consciousness, through the power of the Omni Force.*

Stephen: *Yes.*

Judith: *It is moved by the Great Mysteries. It is moved by the force of the Source of Creation, and this speaks of the Covenant of Humanity, the purpose for human existence, and the fulfillment of the Prophecy of One is ascension.*

Stephen: *Yes. That's exactly what I am writing about.*

Judith: *Holy cow. This spoken affirms the truth of your existence, Stephen.*

Stephen: *Thank you, Judith.*

Judith: *And this brother and sister witness you now, and then set aside any thought forms that may find their way into a mirror that would reflect this in any way be- sides holiest of holy. As it has been spoken, few know who you are; very few know who you are.*

Stephen: *I do, and I want all of us to know who WE are.*

Judith: *And for you to know who you are and be witnessed by Sean and I, who you trust, is important because there are decisions that you must make, and they, in the alter dimensions in the* *power of manifest Creation, this force that you must feel when the Staff of Moses touches the Ark of the Covenant, and it is a prophecy, it is a time that is coming for you. It is an experience that you will feel in your body, but beyond that, it is an illumination of your God self.*

Stephen: *Yes.*

Judith: *And then a force will affect human destiny, not by your action, but by the actions of the powers that be.*

Stephen: *Yes.*

Judith: *For the Prophecy of the Law of One makes way for those forces to move the destinies of humanity, the destiny of mankind into alignment with the perfect purpose of the Eva Adam Kadom, the blueprint for human existence.*

Stephen: *Indeed!*

Judith: *Kadosh, Kadosh, Kadosh, Adonai Tsebayot Yod Hey Vod Hey Yahweh.*

Stephen: *Aho, Kadosh, Kadosh, Kadosh.*

Judith: *Okay.*

Stephen: *Thank you, Judith.*

Judith: *I'm so honored and blessed.*

~

How can we all "rise to the occasion"?

~

To quote UCLA professor, Dr. Valerie Hunt[7], "The definition of consciousness is our ability to relate to the entire universe…The Field." Ironically, The Field is the title to Lynne McTaggart's book[8], which scientifically reveals the recordable influence of our intentions. Even from a very long distance.

These scientific scholars and many other writers and scientists are now proving that as we open to "The Field" we welcome our Receiving Selves (our God Selves), in our electrical-in-nature bodies and our all-knowing souls. We are comprised of billions of atoms, each with protons revolving around a neutron, just like our solar system and universe. We are natural receivers of the electrical charge that manifests as the ever-present Loving Universal Consciousness that we bathe in. Such a connection at this critical time is a great blessing, as it allows us to tune into the Universal Truths, both within our Selves and with our alive and communicative Earth, which is our precious platform that allows us to evolve in bodies. This is how we come into our own, as genius-level Ascended Beings.

The works of Dr. Valerie Hunt and Lynne McTaggart have a parallel in the grand teachings of the ancient Bhagavad Gita which pre-dates the Hebrew calendar, which is now nearly 6,000 years old, and the Christian calendar which is now just over 2000. Please read the following excerpts to feel the grand calling:

---

[7] See alloneera.com/bioenergy to see the human aura on the screen.

[8] The Field by Lynne McTaggart, a fascinating documentary of scientific experiments demonstrates our significant impacts on each other and on nature! The Bhagavad Gita, part of which is reproduced with permission: Krishna to Arjuna: 13:1 this body, Arjuna, is called the field. He who knows this is called the knower of the field.

KRISHNA

1. This body, Arjuna, is called the field. He who knows this is called the knower of the field.

2. Know that I am the knower in all the fields of my creation; and that the wisdom which sees the field and the knower of the field is true wisdom.

3. Hear from me briefly what the field is and how it is, what its changes are and whence each one comes; who is the knower and what is his power.

4. This has been sung by seers of the Vedas in many musical measures of verse; and in great words about Brahman, words of faith and full of truth.

5. The five elements, the thought of 'I', consciousness, subconsciousness, the five powers of feeling and the five of action, the one mind over them, the five fields of sense-perception;

6. Desire, aversion, pleasure, pain, the power of mental unification, intelligence, and courage: this is the field and its modifications.

7. Humbleness, sincerity, harmlessness, forgiveness, uprightness, devotion to the spiritual master, purity, steadiness, self-harmony;

8. Freedom from the lust of the senses, absence of the thought of 'I', perception of the sorrows of birth, death, old age, disease and suffering ;

9. Freedom from the chains of attachments, even from a selfish attachment to one's children, wife, or home ; an ever-present evenness of mind in pleasant or unpleasant events;

10. A single oneness of pure love, of never-straying love for me ; retiring to solitary places and avoiding the noisy multitudes;

11. A constant yearning to know the inner Spirit, and a vision of Truth which gives liberation; this is true wisdom leading to vision. All against this is ignorance.

12. Now I shall tell thee of the End of wisdom. When a man knows this he goes beyond death. It is Brahman, beginningless, supreme: beyond what is and beyond what is not.

13. His hands and feet are everywhere, he has heads and mouths everywhere: he sees all, he hears all. He is in all, and he is.

14. The Light of consciousness comes to him through infinite powers of perception, and yet he is above all these powers. He is beyond all, and yet he supports all. He is beyond the world of matter, and yet he has joy in this world.

15. He is invisible: he cannot be seen. He is far and he is near, he moves and he moves not, he is within all and he is outside all.

16. He is ONE in all, but it seems as if he were many. He supports all beings: from him comes destruction, and from him comes creation.

17. He is the Light of all lights which shines beyond all darkness. It is vision, the end of vision, to be reached by vision, dwelling in the heart of all.

18. I have told thee briefly what is the field, what is wisdom, and what is the End of man's vision. When a man knows this he enters into my Being.

19. Know the Prakriti, Nature, and Purusha, Spirit, are both without beginning, and that temporal changes and Gunas, conditions, come all from nature.

20. Nature is the source of all material things: the maker, the means of making, and the thing made. Spirit is the source of all consciousness which feels pleasure and feels pain.

21. The spirit of man when in nature feels the ever-changing conditions of nature. When he binds himself to things ever-changing, a good or evil fate whirls him round through life-in-death.

22. But the Spirit Supreme in man is beyond fate. He watches, gives blessing, bears all, feels all. He is called the Lord Supreme and the Supreme Soul.

23. He who knows in truth this Spirit and knows nature with its changing conditions, wherever this man may be he is no more whirled round by fate.

24. Some by the Yoga of meditation, and by the grace of the Spirit, see the Spirit in themselves; some by the Yoga of the vision of Truth ; and others by the Yoga of work.

25. And yet there are others who do not know, but they hear from others and adore. They also cross beyond death, because of their devotion to words of Truth.

26. Whatever is born, Arjuna, whether it moves or it moves not, know that it comes from the union of the field and the knower of the field.

27. He who sees that the Lord of all is ever the same in all that is, immortal in the field of mortality - he sees the truth.

28. And when a man sees that the God in himself is the same God in all that is, he hurts not himself by hurting others: then he goes indeed to the highest Path.

29. He who see that all work, everywhere, is only the work of nature; and that the Spirit watches this work - he sees the truth.

30. When a man sees that the infinity of various beings is abiding in the ONE, and is an evolution from the ONE, then he becomes one with Brahman.

31. Beginningless and free from changing conditions, imperishable is the Spirit Supreme. Though he is in the body, not his is the work of the body, and he is pure from the imperfection of all work.

32. Just as the omnipresent ether is pure because intangible, so the Spirit dwelling in matter is pure from the touch of matter.

33. And even as one sun gives light to all things in this world, so the Lord of the field gives light to all his field.

34. Those who with the eye of inner vision see the distinction between the field and the knower of the field, and see the liberation of spirit from matter, they go into the Supreme.

It is we who can bring in the great winds of change, clear the polluted air, and initiate the incredible cleansing of our Earth. It is we who are now scientifically proving that our intentions affect nature and each other in a profound way. Dr. Masuro Emoto has astounded the world with his extensive lab tests using electron microscopes to show the molecular structure of frozen water crystals before and after caressing the water with our intentions of love and gratitude versus yelling obscenities! Lynne McTaggart has also proven the effects of intentions with her life work and there are links to many others who have achieved scientifically proven results, including our own pyramid documentations, which we will expound upon later[9].

As we become aware of the presence of the LUC or "The Field" in this era of receiving, we are beginning to realize that indeed we are unlimited in our potentials. There is no separation; we are all one. We are now returning to our Original Splendid Intention to be the Realized Beings and the Masters that we are. As we unite in gatherings and in the process of a worldwide crescendo of purpose, we begin to create an ever-unfolding and expanding individual and collective orchestration of vast, yet gentle, loving and continuous, flow in the now. Simply put, we are opening our Selves by opening to receiving the constant flow of loving energy that expands our consciousness, leading us to naturally becoming one with our planet, nature and all entities, as conduits or vessels of Holy Spirit.

Let's have a look at some of the other wondrous discoveries that are popping up all over. The book by Paul Hawken, *Blessed Unrest*, describes our present huge momentum to help and heal by millions of people and corporations engaging in countless ways to help others and the planet. The book *Initiation* by Elisabeth Haich takes us back in great detail to the ways of the Pharaohs in an age of Knowing. The book, *The Dream of the Cosmos: A Quest for the Soul* by Anne Baring explores our cultural roots leading to our crisis and gives us a gripping scholarly lifetime study of the growth of human consciousness. The celebrated author Gregg Braden, during his extensive twelve-year study of the most sacred and honored traditions of humankind, has discovered tangible and unprecedented evidence that we are all part of a greater existence. In his book *The God Code: The*

---

[9] See alloneera.com/intention for further information on the work of Dr. Masuro Emoto and Lynne McTaggart, along with our pyramid documentations.

Secret of our Past, the Promise of our Future, Gregg says a coded message has been found within the molecules of life, deep within the DNA in each cell of our bodies. He proposes that our past is about to change through a remarkable discovery linking the Biblical Hebrew alphabet to our genetic code. Could it be Moses' and Jesus' living messages emerging? For me, it is the sound or the vibration of the letters and the words that touch our souls. There are meanings beyond our three-dimensional scope of understanding that these vibrations unleash, and as we open in receivership, they lift us into unlimited dimensions and clarity.

The All One Era is our long-awaited breakthrough. Here, we are opening to receive the ever-present flow of Guidance. As we fulfill this glorious prophecy with a world-wide establishment of connecting gently with each other's bands of energy in gatherings, we celebrate the essence of who we are, who nature is, and how we (and she) magically weave her way back to flourishing in love. These gatherings, celebrating nature at the new and full moons and returning us to our tribal roots of gathering around the fire, are conducive to catapulting our ascension. Catapulting this era as we jointly welcome this state of receivership, we open our electrical-in-nature brains and nervous systems to connect with, fully Know, and be one with the constant flow of energy that surrounds us at all times. This Guidance or Godance transforms each of us from being ego-based (a normal human state) to being conduits of Spirit, as the Knowingness flows through us, invigorating and restoring our health and vitality, and subsequently, all of our environment. As ascended Masters we merge with all there is. We become one with our environment. We ARE the trees, we ARE the rocks we ARE the water, we ARE the air we breathe, we ARE the animals, we ARE the moon, sun. stars and indeed the Earth...NO SEPARATION. There is no time, our consciousness is unlimited and forever, there is no death, we ARE consciousness, the essence Herself. We are electrical vibrational connected OWNERS OF ESSENCE...Energy...$E=MC^2$.

These moon gatherings are honoring the cycles of nature and reuniting us in our Earth's harmony and giving us a physical way to begin our homecoming. While in each other's bands of energy, we are greatly recognizing and enhancing our ability to fully embrace our original sublime purpose, our all-powerful togetherness in love as co-creators. May we now surrender to the glory of the Knowingness that is within us all and that joins us all in "The Field."

~

In 2005, Summerhill Winemaker, Dr. Alan Marks, and I landed in Beijing on business. We were invited to export our organic ice wine to the Peoples Republic of China's military for their annual Lunar New Year celebrations. Upon arrival, we were taken to a highly-secured military base, and then to a nightclub restaurant where we enjoyed a wonderful festive banquet, and had the opportunity to share our ice wine with our generous hosts. It was almost 2:00 a.m. when we finally returned to the hotel and I discovered my room was on the twenty-second floor. Terrified of heights, my only reprieve was the thought that perhaps being at such a high level would allow me to clearly see the night sky.

Perched in front of that twenty-second-story window, I was unable to even see across the street, much less see the stars! In the depths of winter, the air was condensed with thick dark pollution from the burning of coal used as fuel for heat[10]. Concern for the environment and our Earth began to fill every atom of every cell of my being. My heart ached, and I once again heard and felt the echoed cries of humanity and of our beloved animals and plants.

Removing myself from the depressing view and proceeding into the bathroom, I filled the tub with hot water and lit a candle. As I turned off the lights and climbed into the tub, I embraced the breath and experienced instant meditation welcoming Grand Oneness. A magnificent, pulsing, purple light engulfed me and connected me to multiple dimensions. My soul reached out to the unlimited universe and I became one with all there is. In that fraction of a second of absolute clarity, I consciously decided to become an instrument to cleanse the pollution! Tuning into my well-practiced ritual of consciously whisking away clouds, I began blowing away the dense pollution with the intensity of my whole entire being. It was in this moment that I experienced oneness with *The Soul of the World*, taking us all back to the time when our air was pure, species knew no threats of extinction, clean water flowed freely, and we lived in harmony with our Earth.

---

[10] Frightening reports indicate that pollution in Beijing has reached record levels. As stated in a study by Greenpeace, along with Peking University's School of Public Health found that "Last year thousands of premature deaths in Shanghai, Guangzhou, Xi'an, and Beijing could be linked to PM2.5 air pollution."

Raising my arms and offering forth the Sacred Breath, I channeled my intentions from "the Lord God of my being" and envisioned the dark polluted air outside dissipating. The intent resounded in me so powerfully that it rendered me to feverishly stand up, hold out my hands, and spin 'round and 'round. As I stood whirling in a state of profound unity with all there is, I heard the wind begin to fiercely howl. The gale was so powerful that the building began to sway. Ironically, I made no immediate connection between the windstorm and the intentions I had just set; all I could do was stand in awe of the deafening torrent outside. The strong currents escalated throughout the night and into the next day.

Upon entering the hotel lobby in the morning, I watched the doormen struggle to hold the doors open as guests bent down and pushed their way through the wind. Our host arrived to take Alan and me for a walk along the famous Great Wall. The gusts of wind were so fierce that we had to crouch down below the wall and crawl along a small portion of the historical fear-based feat of architecture.

The evening brought calming winds, as throngs of people lined the sidewalks in every direction. For the first time, perhaps in many years, they were able to stand out in the streets, look up at the sky, and see the stars! The thick veil of pollution had dissipated. It was a mighty cleansing! I was filled with a great resurgence of confidence, gratitude and awe. I reflected that indeed we are all conduits and servants. Our full Presence in the *Now* is all we ever need to have. It is by being IN such <u>Presence</u> that we reclaim our power. It is within each and every one of us to behold such extraordinarily powerful experiences!

The Grand Purpose of The All One Era is to welcome the prophetic message that **we are Divine** and can and do have constant impact on all that is; this is the ultimate blessing of this time in our times. We surrender and allow the constant flow of Spirit, absolute love, abundance and peace. When we open to the loving cosmic flow, we influence and create the healing of our Selves and our Earth. **We first need to acknowledge ourselves and realize our worthiness as channels for receiving. This is an ascension welcoming our Knowingness.** We clearly see that individually, and much more strongly as collective groups, we instigate profound change with our powerful intentions. We are ascending to operate from our hearts rather than our minds, to seek truths from our guts rather than our brains, to lead from our loving Selves rather than our ego selves, as we enter into our awakenings, and becoming Realized Beings – one who is one with all, and who acknowledges deeply the energies that surround us at all times. We are Grand Ambassadors in the Now of eternal love. As we receive and take back our power, we know we are, each of us, unlimited immortal Holy Beings.

There is an organic formula for the transition to achieve planetary harmony. The first and foremost truth is to be one with our inner Knowingness and trust this Holy Guidance. This aligns us with our most powerful and splendid state of *Pure Love*. The second is to strive to maintain our bodies as pure vessels through making highest conscious choices that we restore our ultimate physical and planet health and vitality. The third, is to pro-actively share our Self-healing process and our grandness. An excellent avenue is to regularly attend the powerful gatherings which are centered around a sacred fire. The fire acknowledges the Presence of the Grandmothers and the Grandfathers (all our relations), allowing them to come to us through the fire. We direct our meditation and intentions to the fire. Wherever possible, the gatherings should take place in settings that are conducive to group meditation (ideally with a sacred geometry aspect or outdoors). Each of the All One Era gathering branches will be connected to a transparent company leading a revolving Central Council of individuals connected worldwide. The AOE Council has formed an All One Era Certification to ensure that goods and services have heart and Supreme Consciousness and are in harmony with this planet.

We have a grand mission. It is up to each of us to first go within and know ourselves, then to create a vision that is in full alignment with the needs of our planet, and to align ourselves with those who can help us bring it all fully alive. Within our precious bodies we carry our consciousness, our universal Knowingness. Once we "get it," we naturally tune back into that original heritage and intention of our pure, organic nature, and the urgency to expand it worldwide[11]. It is now up to us to "reincorporate" the commercial corporations, giving them heart! Only *going within* restores

---

[11] Nassim Haramien shares his scientific discoveries and his brilliant "connected" perspective on Our True History: alloneera.com/truehistory

harmony and abundance, not politics, economic restraints, threats of war, or giving our power to tyrants or corporations. We all come from tribal beginnings and this lofty awakening is the making of a major grassroots ascension into global peace and harmony. All we need is to proactively be in a state of receiving and have patience, fortitude, conviction, courage, and confidence. Once we have recognized and acknowledged our Eternal (there is no time) Receiving Selves, we become beacons of light to ourselves and instantly to others. Our awareness and our coming together as a conscious collective is now unfolding and we are rapidly opening to receive the constant loving Guidance. We who are laying the foundation are the prophets and emissaries of peace and restoration that we have been waiting for. This IS the Age of Aquarius, the promised Messianic Age, the Christ Consciousness Age and the All One Era of mergence with Loving Universal Consciousness that we ARE – the very cosmic consciousness energy we create from moment to moment, eternally. We are who we've been waiting for. The time is NOW for us to come into our own!

With this global ascension, we become naturally united in being intolerant to atrocities like child abuse, wife beatings and rape, pornography, child slavery, tyrant leaders, nuclear war threats, government corruption, corporate greed, pollution, and any and all fear-based activities. The holistic management of our magnificent planet, the return to our tribal heritage, and our Original Splendid Intentions are naturally and automatically Guiding us to Know that such activities are not in harmony with the nature of our Loving God Selves. While we acknowledge that our drive, relentless ambition, and spirit of competition have brought us to great heights in the creation of technologies, economies, and businesses, they have come at the cost of crippling our planet and crippling the very spirit of humanity. We surely can nurture our Earth and ourselves without this short-sightedness and aggressiveness.

We are ready now to respond to nature's calling for us to open ourselves and to provide her with a cleansing. Like us, she is naturally resilient and healing, and is ready to bounce back. The silver cords that tie us to her, and all there is, have shrunk. We have become more and more oblivious to our polluting, destroying, and ravaging her. Our awakening opens and allows us to embrace and express a gigantic wave of gratitude[12]. She feels and desperately needs this gratitude now, as she so actively displays her cleansing! All she needs are our reinforced silver cords, our renewed soul commitment to being deeply rooted with her, as one with her.

The shift into the All One Era is a time of planet-wide ascension. It is a movement that anyone, of any age, can understand and be one with. We are so fortunate to be in bodies at this most thrilling of all times in our time. A shift! A *total* change! A return home to who we really are! This is our time of opening pure awareness and appreciation, and of our merger with eternity. This is our most glorious time since creation began – a true homecoming. We are reversing the direction of our increasing material pursuits and of living so absorbed in the human drama. Now is the promised renewal of our oneness with all there is and the bringing forth of our brilliant Light, which instantly dispels all darkness that we have allowed to be brought upon ourselves. Selah!

---

[12] alloneera.com/gratitude

The Prophesized Homecoming
The end of the Mayan Calendar. December 21, 2012
The official time of the All One Era Awakening.

The Hopi Prophecy Stone on the Hopi Reservation in Arizona.
Photo Credit: roamingthemind.com

At a Summerhill Pyramid Winter Solstice gathering in December 2016, a beautiful woman
named Mariam spoke of the Tzolkin calendar.
Watch her presentation at: alloneera.com/galacticactivation

*"Imagination is more important
than knowledge.
For knowledge is limited to
all we now know and understand,
while imagination embraces the entire world,
and all there ever will be
to know and understand."*

Albert Einstein

Chapter Three

RISING UP

When do you have day and night at the same time? The answer is twice a day, at sunrise and sunset. These are two of the most colorful and precious times of the day; both of which usually do not get our attention, because we are either asleep or too busy. Connecting directly with the sun, or RAA, is a totally invigorating, physically nourishing, exhilarating experience, especially when standing in bare feet upon the earth. Our star connects us to all the stars and all there is. Sun-gazing titillates our ancient roots and awakens our souls, as part of this connection. You feel the love. You feel the "foreverness" in the present moment. You know that we are connected and Guided.

As the beautiful song goes, "When you wish upon a star, makes no difference who you are, anything your heart desires will come to you." When you look upon a star and emphatically pronounce "From the Lord God of my being, unto the Lord God of your being," the bond between the two of you strengthens; they see you and it is an instant joyous reunion! They yearn to know us and be us, and we yearn to know them and be them. This revelation came to me through my deep appreciation of our star, our sun, our glorious ball of burning gases that travels through the universe. We are in a state of absolute synchronicity, intelligence, and most of all, profound love that we can behold around us at all times. The truth, the inner jolt, is simply that: when we look upon a star, they are looking at us too! They and we *ARE* the essence of life, and perhaps the grandest representation of the highest and most magnificent Holy burning love there is and could ever be. They are ever-evolving in their love and they shine out to us! *US!* We see them, feel them, and know them.

We ARE them! They are US! We are ONE! Our dreams have come true; we are surrounded by love; the stars surround us!

On Easter Sunday evening 2014, during my regular daily practice of sun-gazing (looking directly at the sun for the last half-hour before sunset or for the first half hour at sunrise, when the human eye has zero vulnerability to injury), I had the most magnificent *ah-ha* moment. Standing on the beach in bare feet, in a trance state of glorious oneness with all there is, my soul merged with eternity and was exalted to heights of total bliss, harmony, and all-Knowingness. My body became a timeless vessel filled with exuberance and joy, and I gained immense clarity and perspective. I flashed upon the biblical story of Moses leading the Jewish people out of Egypt, where they had been kept for centuries as slaves.

The story is recounted in Exodus, where the sea parts and the Hebrew people flee to safety before closing and drowning the Pharaoh's advancing army. You may be familiar with the story of how Miriam placed her precious baby brother in a basket after Pharaoh decreed to take the lives of all the first born male Hebrew children. She sent him drifting down the Nile, knowing he would soon be found by one of the Pharaoh's wives, who were bathing downstream. It was the Pharaoh's daughter, Batya (meaning "daughter of God" in Hebrew) who named the baby Moshe (Moses), which in Hebrew means "drawn forth or bring in from the water."[13]

We go on to know the wondrous story of how Moses became a member of the Pharaoh's family and grew up in the palace, where he was indoctrinated into the mysteries of this fully enlightened and highly skilled ancient civilization that dwelled in Egypt for eons. They were the elongated-skulled entities that were one with the sun (RAA!) and all of creation. They felt their eternal connection to Spirit. They Knew they were God. Moses grew up knowing this all-powerful wisdom. He Knew what it was to be *God in a body*. He had become fully initiated as one of the

---

[13] Author Peter Thompkins, in Secrets of the Grand Pyramid, said: "Heliopolis was considered the greatest university in the world. It had existed since much earlier times under the domination of the priests, of whom there were said to be 13,000 in the times of Rameses III, 1225 B.C. More than 200 years earlier, Moses was instructed at Heliopolis 'in all the wisdom of the Egyptians,' which includes physics, arithmetic, geometry, astronomy, medicine, chemistry, geology, meteorology and music."

Living Ascended Masters in the Pharaoh's Palace. He was raised Knowing the universe as one with his complete Self – a total microcosm of the macrocosm. It is now scientifically possible to recognize that one human being has all of the components of the entire universe; that we, individually, are microcosms of the entire macrocosm!

In the moment of my epiphany on the beach, Moses' plight became clear. He was a man who had been initiated into the All One Grand Teachings, in the most sacred ancient mystery schools, where he was immersed in total splendid Holy Oneness. These Grand Teachings are pure. They come through Realized Beings that have come forth in our recent history, the last 10,000 years, through sages like Krishna, Moses and Jesus and also from thousands of others who are with us today, and are always with us, who fully understand, know and love the Divinity that we are. Many of the Grand Teachings are eloquently set forth, though some are also sadly distorted, allowing fear to reign. The Grand Teachings are all around us, though they have been subdued possibly because it was felt that we were not ready for them.

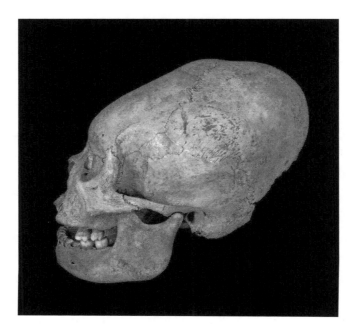

Moses knew he had been born to Hebrew parents and that he had the unique and glorious opportunity to impart his vast, yet elementary wisdoms to his people! You will recall the story of a famous display of magic that dazzled the Pharaoh, as Aaron turned his staff into a serpent and forecast the angel of death taking all the first-born sons of the Pharaoh's people. Moses quickly called for the Hebrew people to paint the blood of an unblemished, sacrificed lamb on their doorposts as a sign, so that the angel of death would <u>pass over</u> their houses and slay only the first born of the Egyptian peoples (Exodus 12:1-28). His prescription worked, as only the first-born sons of the ancient civilization were taken. In horror, the Pharaoh released all the Jewish slaves. Today, Jewish people in all parts of the world celebrate this miracle each year with a dinner known as the <u>Passover</u> Seder, a "freedom from slavery memorial." The Passover Seder, a festive meal featuring unleavened bread to commemorate the forty years of wandering in the desert without ovens to leaven the bread, was celebrated as Jesus' <u>Last Supper</u> before he was taken to the gallows.

It was precisely at this time during <u>The Exodus</u> that Moses realized his plight to now have to enlighten his people and share his experience of Universal Oneness that he had reveled in during his life in the Pharaoh's Palace. How to impart this simple yet vast wisdom to his people? Recalling this was my ah-ha moment! Moses was faced with perhaps the most difficult of all possible challenges.

From all accounts, there were about one million slaves and their families present when Moses led them into the desert, where they were to wander for forty years. In spite of food falling from the sky (manna from heaven) and a host of other miraculous displays, the people failed to grasp Moses' Grand Teachings of their unity with Holy Spirit. Instead, they began making graven images to worship. They were unable to open and allow themselves to align with the all-loving, eternal flow of universal consciousness, and become Realized Beings, as their teacher Moses had. The choice was clear: the people were not ready for such glorious enlightenment. The next best thing he could do for them was to create scriptures and commandments with a fear base. He gave a brilliant concept of one invisible God but a God to be feared which was outside of themselves, as they had obviously lost touch with the Divine Fire within after so long an ordeal in slavery. God would have to be a separate entity to be feared so the people would stay in line versus a love-based merger with

Divine Guidance. This, he Knew, would maintain order and would eventually evolve to alignment with Divine Spirit. He created the famous Ten Commandments, followed by all the scriptures for them to live by. These scriptures, known as the Old Testament or The Five Books of Moses or The Torah were and still are the foundation for the Judeo/Christian era. We see that Moses felt it necessary to teach from a fear-based perspective for his people to unite and find their way to multiply and once again become a nation. His commandments of "Thou shalt not…" versus "Thou art…" Holy instruments of eternal love were blessedly followed three thousand years later by Master Jesus. These teachings are in the New Testament and open the way to return to our all-Knowing Selves. The famous quotes, "Have we not all one Father" and "I and the father are one," signify that both Jesus and Moses shared the same plight and that this was the plight of today up to the dawning of the All One Era.

The question arises: Are we ready for the revelation that indeed we are love and we are Divine Spirit – the *I AM* awareness that instantly opens us as conduits? The Guided work of Moses' commandments and the work of all the scribes are inspirationally crafted, however, they paled for me when I clearly realized that the purity of being in sublime lovingness - as ALL ONE entities - is indeed the ONLY commandment and only scripture that is ever needed. Moses knew that we *ARE* God. The people at that time were just not ready to grasp it. Sun-gazing on this mild, breezy Easter Sunday evening was indeed a grand moment in foreverness for the Christ Energy, and for the all one love message, to come through! Selah!

~

How do we receive and apply our newfound freedoms?

~

I am in awe of the vast scope of what the word *God* has come to represent. While many agree that it is not the long-white-haired old man we see in antique paintings, we continue to cling to stereotypes and images and conjure ideas of a fear-based elder, Creator or Force who we shrivel before in submission. Our current all one era is a blessed time of awakening, where we are reclaiming our power and saying that we embrace the majesty and feeling of *being one with Divinity*. We are not saying we are God, the feared ancient image; we are opening our feminine receiving sides (our X chromosomes) to allow the ever-present cosmic energy to flow through us and for us to become instruments of divine essence in a body.

As a man with XY chromosomes, Y being an aggressive, egoic dominating characteristic, I am aware that we men tend to live by our intellect. If we can't find a reference or a quote from someone else, and if we don't grasp something, we might fake it, or even lie or sweep it under the rug. Surrendering that ego aggressive self, we are opening our feminine X chromosomes to fill us with Guidance. It is simply a little easier for women, as they have XX chromosomes, versus XY for us men. Our receiving happens very subtly, we become Conduits of Spirit. There is a wonderful video called "Today I Rise"[14] showing that women hold the essence of Creation Itself and that we men are blessed to be with them on all levels.

Our All-Oneness and ability to create is reinforced each day, as it spreads exponentially and reaches global proportions. Some part of us knows the existence of our ability to actually BE angels, demonstrating pure love and unity. It is an awareness that comes to us and is further reinforced through the vastly rich experiences of our years of life in the body. The messages weaving themselves through every facet of our days has always been and shall always be that of peace, love, and the expansion of our consciousness, as the ultimate and possibly only avenue to peace, joy, abundance…and rejuvenation.

---

[14] See alloneera.com/todayirise

Reflections

In New York City on April 10, 1944, near the end of World War II, I was born into the world. It was a time of great global chaos. As I entered my human form, many of the world's nations stood in opposition to each other. I was a war baby and one of many births during a time of millions of war-related deaths. It was a time of outrageous behavior for the human race. The first atom bomb test was conducted on July 16, 1945, creating a new paradigm where we, for the first time, held the power to completely annihilate all life on Earth. Upheaval was running rampant, and I endured unprecedented tests of human suffering, as they unfolded before me.

My parents, Leo and Mildred, had met in a swirl of love on a dance floor in Manhattan, and won the dance contest! They immediately discovered that they both were descendants of Jewish families from Kiev, Russia and instantly became engaged. They were beacons of light, both giving of themselves to others with all their hearts. I saw so much love within them. They were both authors, professors and brilliant orators. When not doing worldwide lecture tours or writing text books, using their skills to help educate others, sadly they used some of those same skills against each other. The generous and gentle loving care they extended to the community was not at all paralleled in their attitude toward each other. Bearing witness to these two-great people continuously lashing out at each other, I turned my frustration into crying fits. I hoped with all my heart to deter my parents from the great harm I saw them manifesting. Even as a little boy, I had a deep longing for peace and love. Thrilled with joie de vivre, the "love of life," I wanted to share everything I had inside me with the world. While my crying efforts did allow moments of peace to prevail, they were not nearly enough to end their "war."

One evening, in the early summer of 1957, my three-year-younger sister Valerie and I heard sirens in our neighborhood as we played at friends' houses. All us kids darted to our house to see ambulances, and were witness to my parents lying bloodied on the grass and being taken to be hospitalized. This most violent of all the battles between them had finally torn our family apart. Shortly after my parents' recovery, Val went to live with mom and Grandma Esther in New York City, and I stayed with dad in our suburban home. In that moment, the whole world became my family. It was as if Val and I had been orphaned, setting the stage for my being one with all there is. She pursued a musical career and was surrounded by many friends, but not all were a good influence on her. She went on to achieve her four-year degree and became a public-school music teacher, but soon succumbed to a sad life of tragedy and illness, and an early death. Oddly, her greatest mentor was the world-renowned Wilhelm Reich, who gave her great purpose as she devoted herself to teaching his Orgone Inner Body Breathing Techniques. Serendipitously, his biography was presented in the *New York Times* on the day of Val's funeral in August of 1999.

At thirteen, I began living at my neighbors' houses. The Scalis, D'Onofrios, Pupos and Zuccaros all welcomed me and fed me. "Eat! Your skinny!" became a good laugh every day. I loved them all so much and they taught me true hospitality. I also loved my dad, but although we shared a house together, I was undoubtedly on my own.

On a brick at dad's house, I inscribed "1957" in white paint. I knew then that, within me, I held a monumental scale of messages and contributions, and that the year 1957 should be marked as a crucial turning point. That was the year I knew that the wars and destruction on our Earth must cease. I knew then that by our knowing that we are Forever Beings, we would have and hold our precious heritage, and we would surely end all the world's fighting and strife. I knew we had the wisdom to naturally provide for each other so that we all flourish in peace, happiness, and in ever higher consciousness and bliss. There was great clarity that I do this work and share these messages, and I knew that one day I'd be heard. Since childhood, everything has been so clear to me, with my dreams, visions and meditations further clarifying this Grand Purpose. The bloody events of 1957 spurred great questions about who I was, who all we humans are, and how glorious it is to be in a body in such a splendid, magnificent, vast universe, in spite of facing such daunting circumstances of the times. I feel everyone knows in their heart of hearts that we are all connected, and we created and continue to re-create our all-powerful Selves and our appreciation for all there is.

As a little boy, I began reciting, what was to me, a profound feeling of my oneness in a three-part prayer before going to sleep every night:

I pray to God for peace and happiness on Earth. Amen.
Thank you, God, for everything. Amen.
God bless the world. Amen

We can all now live this prayer, going around consciously blessing the world and everything at all times as if we ARE the God that we pray to. The twenty-two-word prayer resonates and stays with us. In its simplicity, it captures everything, as long as the scope is included that we ARE Divine, the Cosmic Love or Christ Energy, or that we are conduits of the Loving Universal Consciousness and not God as a separate entity. As we progress in our understanding of life, Spirit, God, and Creation Itself, we are *Goded* (Guided) and strive to proactively create peace and happiness on Earth from the core of our BE-ing.

As we touched upon the end of World War II and marked the beginning of the American Dream of home ownership, North America was becoming a haven for expatriates from all over the world. Those of countless backgrounds amalgamated, easing their strict traditions and beliefs and letting go of their heritages with the objective of building a new life together, lifting the dark clouds of the past to create harmony, peace, and happiness. They wanted a world where they could freely express themselves and raise their families in joy – a place where everyone could feel at home, and own a home.

Having been on my own, I was quite independent and had started working as soon as I was eligible at age 13. My paper route provided me with about $3.50 a week, and by tenth grade I had graduated to stocking shelves at the local supermarket and working weekends at the local catering house. At the catering house, I could log over twenty hours in a weekend at $1.05 an hour, plus tips. I was building a nest egg and parlayed it by buying boats and motors, doing restoration work and reselling them. By the time I was in eleventh grade, I owned seventeen boats and had them all in different states of completion and re-sale. In twelfth grade, I met my sweetheart Eileen and we were married just after my graduation on August 1, 1962. I was just eighteen. By my twenty-second birthday, we had built a new lakefront house and had two Cadillacs in the driveway. It seems that being on my own from such an early age had instilled an obsession to be fiercely financially independent. The market was so strong with every young couple striving to own their own home, and I had become the "boy broker" and held the record of making the most home sales in the area.

After years of tremendous success, which included buying and developing land, as well as brokering the sale of houses, land and commercial property, I began to long to have children and be a family man, but sadly Eileen, who had been the oldest of seven, felt she had done her motherly duties taking care or her siblings without too much help from her busy parents. We reluctantly and amicably parted ways after seven happy years. Our parting marked a whole new beginning for me.

A wonderfully joyous and vivacious red-haired, freckled young lady named Annie (who loved children) came into my life serendipitously. Annie and I shared the feeling of absolute ecstasy… "love of life." We were both on the same high in appreciation of having a body. We were enthralled to practice tantric yoga. We also sat in lotus position meditating for many hours at a time, and we were enchanted in teachings from India. I began to leave my beloved Catholic Church and embark on an immersion into ancient Hindu ways, which included living on an austere diet called Macrobiotics, which had been developed in Japan as an ultimate cleansing. These changes stimulated even greater triumphs in my lucrative real estate career as well as building the foundation of a close, healthy, physically and spiritually loving relationship. We were blessed with a son on September 24th, 1971, three and a half years after our meeting date. Matthew David never cried. He was so happy. He would lie in his crib, cooing and chanting, and he'd sleep for twelve hours at a time. He was and is a pure, happy, delightful soul!

Just as Matt was being weaned, Annie, in her ever-independent way, chose to leave us as she saw how close we were and so she could travel to India to be with our guru. Matt and I wanted mom to follow her heart. In 1972, with a signed affidavit from Annie, the court awarded me sole custody and I became the first official single father in the State of New York. Being a single parent taught me so much about being both a father and a mother; a new dimension of what the word love meant for me. I thoroughly enjoyed the magnificent one-on-one father-son joyous interaction and unconditional motherly love. Within that experience came the profound awareness of how unconditional love stays with us forever. Learning how to *be* motherly love and to offer it to others is a gift to ourselves. Learning how to be a father to all, to take the responsibility and the joy is a dimension I proudly have and admire in others. This Fatherly care blossoms in all of us as we ascend in this new Glorious Era! My beautiful boy was love, pure love. We did everything together, and I rarely left his side. The closeness and total bonding we enjoyed brought us both to extreme heights. It was an opportunity I knew all children and parents longed deeply for, and we were both so grateful for having been blessed with the luxury of having such a loving time together.

Through this time of deep introspection, I realized a feeling of profound oneness with everyone and with all of creation. I became one with my sweet little boy and with the enormous responsibility of being a parent. Caring for him made me want to provide the best nutrition, education, air, water, and loving people for him at all times. It was a vision I knew I wanted to extend to the larger community. To do so, I became an activist for ecology on all levels. I was truly blessed by having fathered a life; it revealed so clearly how every new life is subjected to all that exists. This profound understanding propelled me to offer to all of humanity the same love and nurturing I offered to my boy.

We behold our divine eternal purpose when we consciously choose to bring a child onto the planet. We want, with all our hearts, for that planet to be sustainable so that our children and their children can live a joyous, comfortable, radiant life. A beautiful compliment to this sentiment is Chief Dan George's famous quote, **"The only thing the world really needs is for every child to grow up in happiness."**[15]

The profound experiences and the fierce independence developed in my young adulthood made me wiser. I longed to discover and share more, and to launch an ever-far-reaching message to the world. I wanted to become a conduit of love and appreciation. I longed to return to my original soul purpose to be an all-out crusader for the truly divine meaning of love and not just pursue possessions, such as cars, boats, and material wealth and conform to society's constant greed for more of everything.

---

[15] Author, actor and Chief of the Tsleil-Waututh Nation in Vancouver, British Columbia, Chief Dan George, 1899-1981

The full significance of my awareness of my grand purpose came to a forefront one dark rainy night in 1973 when Matthew and I were sleeping in our remote country home. Three armed and masked men broke the window of our front door. I blindly scrambled to the door without my glasses and found a shotgun pointed at my head! The men screamed obscenities and demanded cash. I told them I had none, and they immediately dragged me into the dining room and tied me up with rope so tight that I was bleeding from my wrists and ankles. They then began carrying out all of our possessions to their van. Soon they demanded to know where I kept my valuables, threatening to kill my sleeping son if I didn't tell them!

As I lay on the dining room floor writhing in pain and anguish, I consciously let go of all separation, instantly feeling a glow of warmth surround me. I welcomed the presence of Divine Guidance. A familiar purple glow began to pulsate between my eyebrows, and I felt myself reach out to the entire universe. I shuddered and drew in a deep breath and let out a long, gentle, and confident Oommmm, pushing past my normal exhale breath until I expelled all the air in my tensed body. I drew in another deep breath, felt tingling all over my body and I exhaled fully with all my strength, blowing out through my teeth with a loud hissing sound. I was reaching out with all my heart, soul, mind, and body, and in that moment, I felt myself begin to lift off the floor! I began to levitate, creating a vibration so strong that it triggered the house fire alarm to blare its high-pitched siren. The men ran from the house shouting more obscenities and tore off down the road in their van. I shuffled into the kitchen and found a knife to cut the ropes loose, and then ran upstairs to hug my boy, who was still sleeping peacefully.

In that moment of levitation many dimensions flashed before me and I saw myself touching all the people, animals, fish, trees, mountains, rivers, oceans, sky, stars, and air with my fervent eternal love. From that epiphany moment, I chose to live as a conduit of pure love, unaffected by direction from fear. It was an immediate release, and a sense of pure peace, a blessing that touched not only my heart, but reached out to *every* heart. It was a connection so strong that it now dominates my being at all times. That night, through my levitation experience, I realized that within our Selves we hold the "geniusness" of all creation, indeed the Grandness of all there is.

We decide the level at which this God-Love vibrates within each of us, and within our world. It is we who chose how connected we are to Spirit, and to what degree we wish to vibrate to merge with unlimited dimensions of consciousness. We have separated ourselves from knowing who we really are. We have historically judged ourselves and each other based on judgments, comparisons, and the narrow viewpoints of our peers and their conduct. We have given our power away to fear-based religions and doctrines, and to a plethora of limitations and regulations that we have chosen to adopt.

Masters' teachings and scriptures, some of which have been kept highly secret, can now be revealed. Well known teachings can now be revised to eliminate any fear-based dogma that may have evolved long after they were originally written. There exists an unprecedented opportunity today with our tools of communication, to clarify the original Knowing Messages and merge them with everyone, everywhere. *A Course in Miracles*, inspired through Helen Schucman and expanded upon by Marianne Williamson and others, has opened the vast potentials to uncover these heretofore sealed and protected revelations. We are now ready!

This is our time to finally understand that we are worthy of being in and simultaneously receiving the love stream, leaving behind any judgement of our Selves or others. We are all equal, and we are all Divine entities. This is exactly what all of the Great Teachers, the Ascended Masters, have been saying all these millennia. We can clearly see now how their teachings were not intended to encourage others to worship them as deities, but to bring us to the realization that **we are all deities**. Just as Moses and Jesus knew, once we are love-based, and not fear-based, we live in harmony with the ever-flowing cosmic vibration of the Loving Universal Consciousness. No longer do we then squander our loving energy by acknowledging fear or fear-based sources, demons, or so-called "evil spirits." Universal love consciousness is our dearly welcomed eleventh commandment...Selah!

Levitating Tibetan Monk in the Himalayas.
Photo Credit: Morki Ro

"Love is the essence of consciousness.
Consciousness is an awareness
of the vibratory field,
the subliminal vibration
of the universe."

Dr. Valerie Hunt,
Professor Emeritus, UCLA
and 40-year Professor and Physiology Researcher.

Chapter Four

FIFTH-DIMENSIONAL LOVE

Love *is* that which we are and always will be. It is always here for us to receive and behold; it is the basis of our return to oneness and is a grand refreshment of humanity's soul memory. It is the expression of God in everything and everyone, with God being the eternal loving energy that continues to evolve through all. God and love are cyclical, ever evolving. Love is God and God is love; we cannot have one without the other. Neither is a figure or idol, but rather a consistent energy running through us all and all there is. That God-love IS a living, ever-evolving clarification force we create from moment to moment. It surrounds us as we proactively pour forth our love, we create our lives and all there is from moment to moment. This is a significant revelation that quantum physics has recently confirmed. As we embrace this awareness, reclaiming our power, we realize our Holy Oneness with all there is. As we reach out in love, we immediately achieve majesty, peace, abundance and prosperity.

Love is a term so vastly misunderstood and too often misused. The sentiment extends far beyond a feeling or object of affection. We use the word in the realm of our human drama with a myriad of superficial meanings, in spite of the constant natural yearning to use it from the highest vibrations of our souls. It is the essence of the word, and not the definition or use, which is the glue that ties us all together.

Mother Theresa said, "In this life we cannot do great things. We can only do small things with great love." Our brilliant Beatles and John Lennon and Yoko Ono sang, "All we are saying is give peace a chance," and "Love, Love, Love, all you need is love." Celine Dion and Barbara Streisand express this sentiment so beautifully in their song "Tell Him": "Love will be the gift you give yourself." Whitney Houston captured it magnificently in "The Greatest Love of All", written by Linda Creed: "I found the greatest love of all inside of me." In the All One Era, all we are saying is "give love a chance."

The old saying that "love conquers all" has never rung so true. Love is our unbridled strength, illuminating darkness, and returning us to a state of universal truth with ever-present Guidance. If we were to fuse all the universal truths and all the Great Masters' teachings of the present and past, we would see that the message is clear and simple enough for a child to understand. Our truth is the return to our Original Splendid Intentions, the exuberance of life itself – the little boy or little girl feeling that makes us tingle with joy and jump for joy! We are casting light upon the veils of our former misconceptions. We now feel our oneness with all there is. We allow our intentions to manifest as they reverberate. We proactively and patiently express our essence in our being, in all we say and do. The recognition of Self burst into the glory of ever-expanding <u>Creation</u> the moment we become one with our all-loving Selves.

Within the radiant Presence of God (Goddess) in my Osaka dream, I experienced, with every ounce of my being, a love so powerful and complete, unlike any experience or definition we denote to the word *love* on our three-dimensional plane. Blessed with the privilege and honor of seeing "the face of God" in that dream, I experienced a profound revelation. I saw Her radiating so magnificently that simply by Her Divine Presence, she touched the entirety of the Earth. This Divine Presence is always here for us to align with and know. From the core of Her being I could clearly see a silver cord extending forth, tying us all together as one. It weaves through, empathetically touching all of the three-dimensional universe and multi-dimensional spiritual planes simultaneously. I saw it as a gently streaming light and an eternal bonding, loving energy, connecting all of us, human and animal, with every blade of grass and body of water, and with creation Herself. Standing before Her, I felt within, a sense of urgency, a sense of excitement and profound, everlasting love and joy. Resonating in every energetic molecule of my Self was the truth that indeed, we ARE Forever Beings – all one with God/Spirit, indeed our Grand Selves, carrying the soul memories of all our incarnations. There is no time…there is no beginning, there is no end; we are in the now at all times and what we experience affects our entire universe, and what everyone else experiences affect us. May a clarification of our eternal love in this homecoming era touch the world with the sparkle of a little child's glee. May we all see "the face of God" in our own face and in each other's beautiful faces, Selah!

Larry Dossey, MD says, **"Consciousness research reveals that consciousness is nonlocal or infinite in space and time, therefore in some sense eternal, immortal and one."** [16]

In that same Osaka dream, there was a collective of the faces of apathy, ill health, misery, and emotional turmoil everywhere. It was a state of the world where the level of consciousness cried out for expansion and abounding love. Yet, in simultaneous parallel to the faces of despair was, and always is, the pure celebration of having a body and being alive on this gift we enjoy, our magnificent plane of demonstration. Taking it all in, I sat in wonderment of our human ability to make choices that affect others, manifest every moment, and give and receive great love. To be one with such energy is to carry a *God Love* within us, every day of our lives. God is the glory of our nature, and love upholds that. As John Lennon said, "God is a concept by which we measure our pain," or the bigger the pain, the more God we look for.

The Bhagavad Gita verses 11:51, 11:52, 11:53, 11:54 and 11:55 state:

Arjuna
11:51 When I see thy gentle human face, Krishna, I return to my own nature, and my heart has peace.

Krishna
11:52 Thou hast seen now face to face my form divine so hard to see: for even the gods in heaven ever long to see what thou hast seen.

---

[16] You can view Larry Dossey's talk "Is the Soul Obsolete?" at alloneera.com/immortality

11:53 Not by the Vedas, or an austere life, or gifts to the poor, or ritual offerings can I be seen as thou hast seen me.

11:54 Only by love can men see me, and know me, and come unto me.

11:55 He who works for me, who loves me, whose End Supreme I am, free from attachment to all things, and with love for all creation, he in truth comes un to me.

As I reflect on the composite of all the beautiful faces that I have ever witnessed within the face of God, I am reminded that it is a reflection of the depth of love vibrating from The Soul of the World. To see a familiarity of every beautiful face ever known to me was to come into full awareness that love is simply the Knowingness that surrounds us at all times. It is a comfort and a deep trust in Divine Consciousness, but most of all, it is the heart-centered, all-encompassing feeling that brings us to ultimate presence and unity. It is to realize a state with no separation, where our glorious Original Splendid Intention first manifested. A soul memory of this loving "all-Knowingness" brings us to our heritage to be God/Goddess, to become one with God, to become one with Love.

Being a conduit for universal love comes collectively with empathy for all of humanity. None of us are immune to having our actions go without impact or to be unaffected by what occurs in all parts of our Earth. **We are one with all actions and thoughts.** As harsh as it may sound, we have all been, and are in some part, a thief, a murderer, a rapist, a liar, a cheater or a taker, just as much as we are, at the same time, giving, compassionate, loving ambassadors of glorious Christ-Energy (aka Highest Dimension Consciousness). Grasping this realization removes judgment and opens a new era where Divine vibration resonates and heals. This time is optimum and highly conducive for us men to allow our feminine sides to come through. With our naturally dominating Y chromosome, men are XY, it is a little more difficult for us to receive the LUC, than it is for our beloved XX chromosome Divas, but we can do it!

Part of our Original Splendid Intention is to feel oneness and to allow it to reverberate through our lives. To do so is to be one with our Earth, and to have Her feel us. When we suffer, she feels our pain, just as we feel Hers. The same applies to woes, strife, hurt, sickness, and death; but, we must remain strong, just as She is always resilient. Our proactive pouring forth of our love goes out and is deeply felt. It is perhaps the most significant avenue for our Earth to refresh and for us to refresh.

It is an extraordinary phenomenon that long after communication has ceased between nature and us, or between us and any of the people we touch, the magnetism, emotion, and power of the connection that was established lingers on. It is this vibration, an energetic silver cord vibration that gives us the opportunity to offer it proactively to others and to all there is, in infinite expansion. For example, our emphatic love for one plant can be shared with all plants. Our love for one person can be extended to all people. Love is boundless in its potential; it is the foundation of the silver cord linking us to all-Knowing and all-loving consciousness. It is a momentum and an everlasting charge, running through the currents of the world. More than a feeling, it connects us all. Here, within our very existence, is all there is. Connecting ourselves with the universal silver cord is to know that we are in a reciprocal world.

By surrendering and allowing our X chromosomes to expand our consciousness, we are instantly one with Loving Universal Consciousness. We welcome the universal truth of freedom from attachments, and love for all creation. To actually feel and know the whole world, we merely need to open ourselves to receiving. As we allow in cosmic vibrations, our wisdom and soul memories begin to flow through us, and we become conduits of the loving light touching all there is in our genius forever unlimited energy. As we shine forth our soul experiences, our actions and intentions affect the entire world, physically uplifting ourselves, our Earth and all there is.

We are spiritual fifth-dimensional beings having a human experience. To come to this realization is to free ourselves from our three-dimensional world of drama, fear, destruction, and illusion. To remove ourselves from that which we think we are, is to bring home the truth and soul memory of who we actually are.

Knowing fifth-dimensional love is to think, feel, and Be God. It is to hold our own power, and not give it away. It is to know that we have been alive forever and always shall be alive. It is to daily proclaim a toast with pure water to life! For ever and ever and ever! *L'Chiam!* It is to know that indeed, we co-created this universe and indeed, we are the essence of life that stems from the essence of love. Love is the essence of Divine Knowingness, and Divine Knowingness is the essence of all there is. There is no judgement of right or wrong, there is only one Holy Guidance and Love.

"One of the greatest gifts of the Fifth Dimension will be the joyous and loving relationships that you will create and enjoy as awakened beings. These unions will be about serving the planet in a state of joyous harmony where the two become one in their commitment to their work as light beings on the planet." [17]

Celia Fenn, Ma, PhD, Author and Channel

In 1977, I was actively involved in the building industry in the flourishing suburbs of NYC, Westchester County. As a member of the Builder's Institute, I was attending a seminar introducing an innovative type of financing. Everyone who was a member showed up that night; it was the most crowded I had ever seen the huge ballroom. Wendy Weiss, the lovely Assistant to the Executive Director of the Builder's Institute, couldn't find a seat for dinner, with the exception of the only vacant one beside me! I had only ever spoken to her on the phone, but the moment she sat down next to me, we both felt the jolt of our bands of energy merging. The classic song "Some enchanted evening" by Oscar Hammerstein became our song! "Some enchanted evening, you may see a stranger across a crowded room. And somehow you know, you know even then, that somewhere

---

[17] Christ energy is a term widely accepted to reference the teachings of the Master Jesus. However, the term can also apply to the divinity within us all. The Master's quote "I and the Father are one," says it all: the I AM.

you'll see her again and again. … Once you have found her, never let her go. Once you have found her never let her go." I invited her for coffee at my house that evening. I was so excited that I drove past my exit and was late for our rendezvous! We were both nervous and so happy! The rest, as they say, is history.

I knew I could trust Wendy and that she trusted me. Love is trust and trust is love. We felt at home with each other and in alignment with universal truths and Guidance which we shared. My six years of joyful single fatherhood ended and a glorious new beginning emerged as together Matthew David and I welcomed our loving Wendy in a beautiful garden wedding ceremony on the lawn of our Bedford, New York home. Sons, Gabriel, Ezra, and Ari were born in quick succession and, like Matthew, they each looked like wise little men from the day they were born! Today, all four are accomplished musicians as The Oot n' Oots, a children's music band, as well as helping me build a model of "man and nature" at our organic winery and bistro in Kelowna, British Columbia.

Chief Dan George said it best in his quote, **"Touch a child, they are my people."** The time we spend one-on-one with a child is so precious, because it is the melding of the two beings as one. By being one with a child, we become that child and are able to step into their life, so to speak. More importantly, when we behold the essence of a child's love, that love can then be extended out to all children. We share the joys of their lives, allow them into ours, and discover that they are one with us. It is my aim to always be spontaneous and child-like. My four sons and darling daughter Esther Ehisa (EE), and my six grandchildren, Abbey, Sophia, Akivah, Eleorah, Ruth and Uma and I dance barefoot on the Earth every moment we are together. I rejoice in their lives, as if rejoicing for the spontaneity of all life in the world. I cherish the spontaneity of all children. To be one in love with all there is, is to understand core-felt exuberance. It is our "little boy" or "little girl" Selves, our precious connection to the ever-joyful Spirit, the thrill of being alive! As Enigma said in their song "Return to Innocence," "That's not the beginning of the end; that's the return to yourself, the return to innocence." This sentiment also reminds us that relationships are the golden threads that link us all as one and always shall. **Love never dies**.[18]

---

[18] alloneera.com/soulmates

The genius level of children thrills me. We can all think outside the box, live in the moment, and Be brilliant and unlimited! Many children are demonstrating what we now term as superhuman feats and expanded superhuman wisdoms. In reality, we all have these abilities.

The Indigo Children, New Children, Star Children, or Gifted Children are a phenomenon in this era. A great honor was bestowed upon me on February 4, 2004, when I was called up to be <u>A Friend of the United Nations</u>, alongside Yoko Ono and His Holiness the Dalai Lama and other esteemed artists and celebrities, for my work with the Indigo Children[19]. For years, I worked with James Twyman and Sharon Williams, expounding the many blessings of nurturing the New Children, our true gifts from heaven![20] Part of the exhilarating experience involved hosting workshops for mothers and fathers of Indigo Children. We worked together to instill changes in current education standards to encourage the children's freedom of expression and their ability to share their gifts. This work is helping to alleviate the sad practices of medicating and sedating these children so they "conform" and behave. These children are here to remind us that we are all brilliant beings. They lead us on an alignment with the Loving Universal Consciousness that we are all a part of.

The absolute child-like joy of being alive in a body is the ultimate thrill and ultimate reverberance that unites us all! It is our Earth upon which we dance, from which we nurture ourselves, and in whose space, we create new life and love. It is our playground, our plane of demonstration, and our precious place where we become physical and able to experience the density of matter, so that we may evolve in our souls.

Individuality is our grandest achievement! Each of us strive to be all we can be! "Vive la différence" – savor and celebrate each and every one of us as together we are one, brilliant, ever-evolving, loving, co-creative force. Remember what Obi Wan Kenobi said in Star Wars, "Stay on target. Use the force, Luke."

---

[19] Please see the Global Vision for Peace 2004 awards at alloneera.com/gvp2004

[20] Learn more at alloneera.com/indigo

*"One of our biggest challenges is to accept and acknowledge our own
greatness and the greatness of others."*
Dr. Valerie Hunt, UCLA Professor

*"Concerning matter, we have been all wrong. What we have called matter is energy, whose
vibration has been so lowered as to be perceptible to the senses. There is no matter."*
Albert Einstein

This quote from Dr. Hunt, alongside Einstein's most famous quote, brings us to the awareness that as we each ascend, we are both matter as physical beings and simultaneously, we are pure energy! As we each ascend into our multi-dimensional Selves, we become a <u>Realized Being</u>. Our power is unlimited and all encompassing.

Today, in reflection of that most profound revelation, I can say that allowing in the energy of multi-dimensional love requires proactive openness and surrender on our parts. We become hollow vessels, open to the highest good and purest love. In doing so, we live on this Earth plane with a wholly new perspective, one where our every action and will is echoed to all others, and theirs to us. We blend our spiritual awareness with our human experience. When we do anything, we are doing it as if it is touching the whole world. If we take a breath, we are thankful for it, as we are breathing for all of humanity. If we eat a meal or drink water, we are grateful and wish abundant food and clean water for everyone. When we learn, we bless the wisdom and extend it forward to all others. And in bringing new life into this world, in the purity of love, we are extending the reach of the silver cord that connects us all.

To be in the space of fifth-dimensional love is to live in a state of being of service on a grand scale. Our human world so often portrays love to be that which is grounded in the third dimension, focused on one another or cast upon an idol. Our love therein becomes a sentiment taunted by the ebb and flow of passion and frustration. The truth of our Knowingness is that we do not want or need to follow one person or idol, because there are none among us who are any greater than the other. We are each none other than servants to the grander whole and to the greatest good of all.

The love we offer is that which we receive as spiritual beings, forever opening ourselves to an ebb and flow of supportive, vast, all-creating energy. In this time of rapid ascension, it is becoming easier to surrender our ego-selves and create lives that align with our service to the whole, offering forth pure love. Through the creation of a network of All One Era gathering venues[21] , all support services and worldly collaborations will flourish. We can fully unite as one in support of the expansion of our consciousness and protection of our planet. We can thrive without destruction, attachment, or unnecessary harm, through our return to a state of natural unity in consciousness.

The phenomenon has begun. We are all now becoming aware that we are conduits and we are starting to speak from our Spirit Selves. We no longer feel the pressure of having to force our aggressive voices or actions from our ego selves. We are beginning to relax a very long state of hysteria and open up to being *Goded* (Guided). Acknowledgment of the ever-present Guidance comes to us in meditation, yoga, conscious diet, many healing modalities, sacred breathing, sacred geometry, and a return to our tribal roots of gathering around the sacred fire[22]. It illuminates our mighty call to action to save our precious creation at this most crucial of all times in our time.

Simultaneously, we are beginning to re-align our interactions with nature – our Earth, moon, sun, and our neighbors beyond the sun. It is a time when all that was complex and fear-based regains its simplicity, and all denominations fuse lovingly as one. Through our celebrations of the moon cycles and the seasonal cycles, and the great outdoors and the bountiful nature of our plants and animals, the whole Earth is reconnected and begins to rise in her vibration.

The actual electrical pulses of nature serve to unite us. As we become receivers and conduits, and no longer just ego-messengers caught up in the allurement of our senses and in our illusions in the human drama, we begin to see and feel the pulses – the aura of nature. The essential messages of the words of all of the Masters, past and present, come together in unity as a single prophecy of

---

[21] See alloneera.com/gatherings

[22] A sacred fire differs from a "regular fire" in acknowledgment that indeed the "Grandmothers and Grandfathers" AKA as "All Our Relations" AKA those on "the other side" come through the fire to us as we revere the fire as a Holy vessel, feeding it with food, water, tobacco and most of all our reverence and our pure intentions.

prophecies now. This call to come together as one is a refreshing, urgently needed look at who we really are. Our connectedness to pure love at every moment releases us from being trapped in a physical body, and catapults us to being ecstatic to have a body. We are one with all there is!

"Once you reach the vibration of the fifth-dimensional human being, you are in
a state of amnesty and light
because the fifth dimension is the world that is safe.
We are in the vibration of that light now."
Judith K. Moore

We are so much more than our three-dimensional existence. Upon having touched the majesty of the fifth dimension and beyond, it becomes almost a chore to function in the third dimension. Once we release the bondage of our physical plane, we soar without limitations. We cannot create the freedom our souls yearn for with our former judgmental doctrines; we end up chasing material things and frustrating ourselves. Freedom is possible perhaps only in the fifth dimension and beyond, because it is there that we capture the feeling of "foreverness" in the present moment and touch upon our infinite potential. The wondrous era of enlightenment and unified conscious alignment is now upon us and we, by embracing our love and the love that surrounds us, are all now ascending, just as prophesized.

The extension of our love, of course, includes all of life, not just the almost eight billion of us humans on our planet. We are reaching out to include all the animals, plants, trees, waterways, oceans, fish, rocks, mountains, and deserts. As we ascend into this Grand State of Receivership, we will all be remembering and cherishing our instinctive pure joy, peace, and happiness, and will simultaneously no longer tolerate ego-driven aggression, cruelty, greediness, and physical destruction.

The rustle of the wind, the growth of plants, and the cries of populations around the planet resonate within each of us. To experience the true depths of fifth-dimensional love is to hear the love we pour into our music making, to smell the aroma of the love we pour into our wine making and cooking, to feel the love we have for each other in love-making, to speak and whisper the love we have for nature, and to shriek out our exultation to be alive when we smell the fresh air from the lush green trees. We pull the moon, our enchantress, into our bodies, under our rib cages, and into our organs, and feel her pulse with our every heartbeat, moving through our cycles and her cycles, because the moon IS us. We are the sun, the planets, and all the constellations. They call to us, we call to them, we feel them, and they feel us. We realize the universe's complexity and yet also the simplicity, as it is brilliantly reflected within each of us. We are conduits of all universal loving energy, and can now, at long last, joyously come together to amplify our possibilities to heal our glorious Earth and, simultaneously, our glorious Selves.

In greater and greater numbers, we exponentially are sensing the energy, vibration, joy, and confidence to achieve unlimited potentials and to collectively acknowledge multi dimensions. We are now, for the first time in eons, opening to receiving the loving Knowingness, this all-vitalizing oneness, this consciousness, this glorious state that has existed and exists always within each of us and within every atom in the world.

"The God-Man consciously manifests and controls all seven levels of creation. But his consciousness identifies itself only with the seventh, divine plane, not with the lower ones. He knows them, masters them, uses them—but does not eat of these fruits of the tree of knowledge of good and evil! He consciously remains in God, in the paradisiacal state. He unites within himself all seven planes in divine unity; he is matter, has a body, is a plant: he animates, nourishes and cares for his body as for a good instrument. He is animal: he has instincts and feelings; he is man: he has intellect and the power of logical thought; he is a genius; he has intuition and works out of the plane of causes; he is a prophet: he stands above time and space, seeing the future and the past, loving the entire universe with selfless, all-inclusive love, helping all creatures towards redemption from the fetters of the world; and he is a God-man: he is omniscient and omnipotent; he is what he is, the eternal being, life itself, God!"
Elisabeth Haich, Initiation

Reflections

Please join me on a reflection to my first visit to Jerusalem in 1983. I had returned to Judaism with the most enthusiasm I had ever felt. I had joined the United Jewish Appeal (UJA) and was attending rallies to raise money for Israel. I was active as the President of the Men's Club in a flourishing Westchester Synagogue, where I met an Israeli architect who had a brilliant blueprint to rebuild the historic Hurva Temple in Jerusalem by preserving its original state in ruins and replacing the partly crumbled original stone walls with glass on top of the ruins, preserving them for all time. At that time, Rabbi Yaakov Rone, our strong leader, had just invited me to accompany him on a trip to Jerusalem to vacate his parent's apartment after they had both sadly passed over. I had not visited Jerusalem, and my excitement built as I was presented with the opportunity to visit the Holy land – the place where, miraculously, the almost-extinct conversational Hebrew language had been revived and declared the official language.

Rabbi took me to the Wailing Wall (the outside Eastern Wall of King David's Holy Temple). There, Jews from all over the world came to pray. However, they were not allowed access to the Holy Temple Mount, where the Islamic Mosque now stands. I immediately flashed on the irony that the religion of Islam was born from the same father (Abraham) as the religion of Judaism. I knew that the prophet Abraham had two wives and that from Sarah, the Hebrew Nation was formed, and from Hagar, the Islamic Nation was formed. I couldn't help feeling a great calling to go onto the Temple Mount to experience the two religions that now held so much tension between them.

To the great surprise of Rabbi Rone, I disguised myself and joined the throngs of Muslim congregants climbing the steps to the sacred mount. I felt the exhilaration rushing into every cell in my body! I took out my camera and began taking three-hundred-and-sixty-degree photographs in an attempt to capture the bursting aliveness of the visible waves of energy before my eyes, but the camera could not capture it. As I was walking slowly toward the Mosque, I was overcome by *Godance* that I was on Holy ground. I felt the need to immediately remove my sandals. I was then pulled around, as if by invisible strong hands, to face East, and began chanting the most sacred Hebrew prayer, The Shema, in Hebrew.

שְׁמַע יִשְׂרָאֵל יְיָ אֱלֹהֵינוּ יְיָ אֶחָד

Shema Yisrael, Adonai eloheinu, Adonai eḥad

Hear O Israel, the Lord our God, the Lord is One.

בָּרוּךְ שֵׁם כְּבוֹד מַלְכוּתוֹ לְעוֹלָם וָעֶד

Barukh shem kvod malkhuto l'olam va'ed.

Blessed be the name of His Glorious kingdom for ever and ever.

וְאָהַבְתָּ אֵת יְיָ אֱלֹהֶיךָ בְּכָל לְבָבְךָ וּבְכָל נַפְשְׁךָ וּבְכָל מְאֹדֶךָ

V'ahav'ta eit Adonai Elohekha b'khol l'vav'kha uv'khol naf'sh'kha uv'khol m'odekha.

And you shall love the Lord your God with all your heart and with all your soul and with all your might.

וְהָיוּ הַדְּבָרִים הָאֵלֶּה אֲשֶׁר אָנֹכִי מְצַוְּךָ הַיּוֹם עַל לְבָבֶךָ

V'hayu had'varim ha'eileh asher anokhi m'tzav'kha hayom al l'vavekha.

And these words that I command you today shall be in your heart.

וְשִׁנַּנְתָּם לְבָנֶיךָ וְדִבַּרְתָּ בָּם

V'shinan'tam l'vanekha v'dibar'ta bam

And you shall teach them diligently to your children, and you shall speak of them

בְּשִׁבְתְּךָ בְּבֵיתֶךָ וּבְלֶכְתְּךָ בַדֶּרֶךְ וּבְשָׁכְבְּךָ וּבְקוּמֶךָ

b'shiv't'kha b'veitekha uv'lekh't'kha vaderekh uv'shakh'b'kha uv'kumekha

when you sit at home, and when you walk along the way, and when you lie down and when you rise up.

וּקְשַׁרְתָּם לְאוֹת עַל יָדֶךָ וְהָיוּ לְטֹטָפֹת בֵּין עֵינֶיךָ

Uk'shar'tam l'ot al yadekha v'hayu l'totafot bein einekha.

And you shall bind them as a sign on your hand, and they shall be for frontlets between your eyes.

וּכְתַבְתָּם עַל מְזֻזוֹת בֵּיתֶךָ וּבִשְׁעָרֶיךָ

Ukh'tav'tam al m'zuzot beitekha uvish'arekha.

And you shall write them on the doorposts of your house and on your gates.

My heart jumped suddenly when two armed guards came rushing up from behind me. They lifted me up by my elbows and escorted me off the Temple Mount, shouting at me in Arabic, "Get off! Get off!" To this day, I continue to ponder the question of our relationship between a force or a deity, a powerful existence outside ourselves that is yet so a part of ourselves. What was it that physically swung me around, making me face East? What was it that made me take off my sandals and chant in Hebrew? What was it welcoming me to this vortex of energy, this "heart of the planet" so to speak, with its torrent of constant controversy and yet, sadly, the current capitol of "spirituality"?

As an aside, if we carefully look at the words of The Shema and listen to them (as words have a distinct vibration), we may actually see and feel the essence. Ironically, the Kabbalistic interpretation, or in other words, the sum of the numerical value of the letters of this daily prayer come out to be humanity's oneness with creation: the number thirteen.

According to Philip Shepherd, **"There is a good reason that we talk about 'gut instinct.' If cranial thinking sets us apart from the world, the thinking in the belly joins us to it. If the cranial brain believes itself surrounded by a knowable world that can be controlled, the brain in our belly is in touch with the world's mystery. The fact that the second brain has been discovered, forgotten, and rediscovered by medicine three times in the past century suggests**

how complicated our relationship with our bodily intelligence is."[23]

Recognizing the constant synchronicities and the spontaneity, the dreams that guide us and the circumstances that teach us, we enter into realization of our unlimited genius. We are no longer amused by the coincidences; we are in tune and spontaneous with them. We become one with them and welcome our spiritual Presence and acknowledge our sphere of influence, which is unlimited. For instance, we acknowledge a cat that walks across the floor and gently caresses us at just the right moment, the radio talk show heard in the car that changes our life with a few revealing words shared across the airwaves while we're sitting at a red light, the little girl who jumps with glee just as you come to visit her, or the special needs person who stops us on the street blurting out a seemingly random line. We come full circle to that which our souls have always known and we so clearly knew at birth: that we are *Goded*, and all we ever need, is to be aware of the ways the *Godance* constantly comes to us and through us.

The present dire state of our Mother Earth is directly related to our having stepped out of our Knowingness that She is one with us. As we acknowledge the present pervading fear for her survival and therefore, for our own, we come into full awareness that it is perhaps only love of all there is, in all its holiness, that will save us. While prayers, even the holiest of them, offer comfort and a stimulation of our natural human trait of wanting to give, this is the time for us to actually feel the essence of love in the words of the prayers we utter, and most importantly, to project our entire Selves into their meaning. For example, one of the holiest of Ancient Hebrew prayers, where the congregants must stand in reverence is the Kadosh. In Hebrew, it is recited:

קָדוֹשׁ קָדוֹשׁ קָדוֹשׁ ה 'צְבָאוֹת מְלֹא כָל הָאָרֶץ כְּבוֹדו

Kadosh, Kadosh, Kadosh, Adonai tzevaot. Melo khol ha'aretz kevodo.

---

[23] alloneera.com/bellybrain. A direct follow-through and compliment to the Grand Teachings of Paramahansa Yogananda (1893-1952) and his ever-flourishing Self Realization Fellowship

It is recited three times with three long Amens after each time. The English translation is *Holy, Holy, Holy is the Lord of Hosts. The Whole Earth is full of His Glory*. Today, this prayer is becoming inter-denominational and recited to bless our highest intentions. The Kabalistic codes reveal that the actual sounds of the words hold a vibration, and that the numbers associated with each of the Hebrew letters that make up the prayer, coincide with (the number) One! Interestingly, the other single most recited prayer in Judaism is The Shema. It is said facing East, morning, noon, and night, and upon your last, dying breath. The Kabalistic code of the summation of the Hebrew letters is also the number One! One invisible God, one universally connected Holy <u>Creation</u>.

If we were to boldly re-write the two most revered ancient Hebrew prayers, today, the changes would dramatically increase the jolt or the feeling of our oneness when we recite them:

The Kadosh

Repeats 3 times

Holy Holy Holy is the Lord of Hosts
The Whole World is Filled with His Glory becomes:

<u>*Holy Holy Holy is the Lord of Hosts*</u>
<u>*The Whole World is Filled with Our Glory*</u>

<u>*Amen*</u>
<u>*Amen*</u>
<u>*Amen*</u>

The Shema

Hear Oh Israel

The Lord Our God

The Lord is One   becomes:

<u>Hear Oh Universe</u>

<u>Holy Eternal Loving Consciousness</u>

<u>Our Love is ONE</u>

The basic difference is that our prayers become an affirmation of powerful purpose, rather than just another extension of giving away our power. For so long, we have given away our power, and we and our Earth have suffered. We have been conforming to our society and the basic belief system that our thinking is everything. We have, at the cost of our freedom, chosen to give away or suppress the love that surrounds us at all times. While we remain naturally respectful, kind, and law-abiding, this is our glorious time to behold our Oneness with all there is! It is an opportunity to be free of the myriad of laws and expectations of society and to experience an organic life of true joy and spontaneity. We have within ourselves all that we require to flourish and heal our world. When we stay centered in our Grand Selves, the seat of our Original Splendid Intention, and to behold the Master within us, we return home to whom we really are as beings unlimited in our potential, flourishing as *one* with the Earth all thereon, and all there is! Here on our plane of demonstration, we are able to know and love ourselves in our Holy bodies. This precious planet, with its ideal living conditions, allows us to individually evolve our souls. We are blessed indeed to have this glorious opportunity. We are blessed indeed to now come together and celebrate our unlimited abundance. We are all each other's teachers and everyone has a gift to radiate to the whole. The age of fear-based conformity is ending. This is the wondrous opening we have always had lying dormant – our awakening to our Forever Selves, our Loving God Selves.

How do we see and share this excitement, this love of life everlasting, with others…with those who are trapped in seriousness and all wrapped up in "the human drama" and materialism?

Now, for the first time in history, we have the two most powerful tools in our hands:

➢ First, the profound, scientifically measurable impact of our conscious intentions, especially when shared in an intentional group experience.

➢ Second, the mighty computer technology in place to further implement our intentions and unite humanity.

As connected Beings – Holy instruments of loving spirit – we hug the earth and roll in her with reverence and joy! We dance bare foot on her, sing to the moon and make eye and soul-contact with the sun at dawn and dusk! The time is NOW to connect with each other and unite to save our planet, and us. In this era, we awaken our dormant Splendid Intentions, and join an ever-expanding universe bathed in love.

Once we see the radiant fifth-dimensional light within ourselves, our Py Ra Mid (pyramid), our fire in the middle, our Holy life force energy, that mirrors the shape of a py-ra-mid (fire in the middle), we start seeing it in all others. Our breakthrough as adult humans, and as and through our children, is a return to this state of full understanding of oneness with all. Mortal fears melt away as we rejoice. We all know that darkness always gives way to light, just as exuding peace and love always overcome worry, anger, and destruction. This is our foundation to realize a great revelation that there are none we can't reach. When we "vibrate" in the fifth dimension and beyond, there is no time and there are no limitations. We easily tap into a fellow receptive entity that holds the capacity to receive. We develop that receivership by allowing ourselves to become conduits and to proactively co-create life around us, even the plants and animals. The conscious creation of our lives is a joyous plane we realize by feeling, seeing, Knowing, and *Being* one with all there is and being in the Loving Universal Consciousness at all times. We ARE The Soul of the World!

BIOENERGY

AURIC FIELD DEMO
WITH DR. VALERIE V. HUNT

Dr. Valerie Hunt served as a physiological science professor at UCLA for over forty years. Born in 1916 to two university professors, she was perhaps destined to be an academic. Before that would come to be, she had a profound mystical experience as a child. After becoming severely ill at the age of eight, she fell into a coma.

During this time, she received direction to be a "Messenger of God."

Upon awakening from her coma, she could miraculously speak five languages.

In the 1970s, Hunt investigated the nature of the electro-magnetic field generated by human beings in relationship to their environments. Using EEG telemetry techniques (hitherto only used by NASA), she was perhaps the first scientist to not only record subjects while trans-dancing, but to discover that humans were capable of generating electro-magnetic fields whose frequencies were many thousands of times higher than previously recorded.

She also observed how the vibratory auric fields we gave off, either expanded or contracted depending on our state of being and our immediate surrounding influences.

Over time, Hunt not only discovered her own innate ability to intuitively tune into these energy states without the need of any recording equipment, but her own ability to communicate with those in a coma or those who had passed away, to help them heal or resolve certain issues. In so doing, she also came to realize that the predominant biochemical model now used in mainstream medicine is limited in what it can offer, and that we need to supplement medical diagnostics and treatments with a more holistic bio-energetic view.

A genius of our time. Dr. Hunt gifted the world with her computer-enhanced technology, showing our aura on a screen. See it now at alloneera.com/bioenergy

"We are not these bodies.
We are Holy
all one forever beings.
As soon as we take off the pressure of thinking
that our bodies are us they heal perfectly."

Stephen Cipes

Chapter Five

REALITY OF ILLUSION

It was in the early evening on a crisp fall day in 2005 when I found myself blissfully alone in the womb-like, earth-covered Summerhill Kekuli slipping into a deep trance state. I had built a huge rumbling fire that cast away the cold from the approaching winter. A brisk wind was blowing in through the flapping bearskin entrance, where I could catch the aura of colors brilliantly pulsating off the swaying trees. As I sat directly on the dirt floor, the dancing vibrant hues of the fire had me entranced, feeling wholly as one with all of the natural world. The connection was so intense that I didn't want to move, not even to take care of the growing need to relieve myself! With every ounce of my being, I attempted to stay totally still, but after much rustling, I arose and wandered outside to the loudly rushing brook. It wasn't my intention to stop right there, but a force much greater than me took over and I immediately fell on the Earth. I completely forgot why I had stepped outside! I rolled over and could see the aura of energy radiating wildly from the plants and trees along the brook. I could see a powerful silver rim of energy rising above the water! Overcome with a primal instinct to be raw in my mergence with the pulsing glowing, abounding nature, I removed all of my clothing, and began rolling in the Earth, embracing *her*. I even took a little piece of the Earth into my mouth and savored it!

Returning to the Kekuli, naked and feeling light and transparent, I embraced the intense oneness-vibration and immediately crouched into the fetal position on the dirt floor. The dazzling energies and dancing in vivid colors continued to pulsate before my closed eyes, and I felt my body releasing like never before. Emptying my bowls and bladder and vomiting all that was in my stomach with a great convulsive moan, I surrendered completely. As the evening darkness spread across the land and the fire dwindled to embers, my breath became silent, and with my face nestled into the earth, I died.

At the moment of my death, I so clearly saw that I was not who I thought I was. Any and all judgments of the person I once saw myself to be were immediately cast away. It was only for a flash that I left the human plane, yet the impact of being in that space left a permanent impression on my soul. The peace, relief and bliss were so inviting. I wanted to stay there forever. A calling deep within me pervaded and as I sat up and reached for blankets to cover my chilled body, I was in extreme appreciation for my every breath. Slowly moving once again, I curled up and slept until dawn. It was a sleep of the most profoundly peaceful magnitude. While not the first time I had received a complete cleansing of my mind, body and soul, this experience differed vastly. In earlier occurrences, I had not completely detached from the material plane, thereby slipping back into my ego self and returning to boast about achievements or about petty human drama details. This time was different. I had changed. I had embraced death, welcomed it, and actively reveled in its sublime state. I had actually seen the ever-pulsating vitality and magnificence in all of nature, and had elevated my perception of my own body, and therefore of all others and of all life! It took great courage for me to have made the choice to stay in the body. Death is so heavenly, inviting, fulfilling, glorious, comforting, light, airy, delicious, beautiful and loving!

I admire hospice aids who lovingly coach those who are passing over. The preparation to make the transition between so-called "life" and so-called "death" is kin to the wise coaching delivered to expectant mothers: the calmer they are, the less pain they will endure during childbirth. I have come to fully understand there is nothing to fear in death, because it is simply our transitioning into a different energy. The more openminded we are to death, the less painful, and subsequently the more glorious, the transition will be. We can now envision ourselves as being welcomers of souls crossing over as we ascend to being in the fifth dimension and beyond in body.

In the fifth dimension, we are Forever Beings, on all "sides" simultaneously. In this long-awaited time in our times, we are finally collectively realizing that we have restricted and lowered our consciousness in bodies. We subdued our vast awareness and our ecstatic state of shared oneness and gratitude by comparing, judging and limiting our Selves to the extent of our collective experiences. We have, up until now, based our very consciousness on our five senses and on our rickety platform of shared experiences. We live in the everyday illusion of that which we think we are. We know better. We are freed in our Knowingness! While there ARE grand truths to behold in our many illusions, we can now unite as one in the grander scenario of each of us breaking through the veil of limitation and becoming a "God in a body," welcoming our multi-dimensional Divinity and our Grand Purpose. There is urgency to make this leap of faith for now, of all times in our time, we stand upon the threshold of utter destruction as never before.

We think we are as we have been conditioned to be in three main categories:
1. Our childhood (The formative years)
2. Our sentiment toward the word "God" (Our upbringing and influences)
3. Our relationships (The levels of soul sharing from and to others)

Our childhood years determine how we feel about ourselves, fashion our future relationships, hold anger, have appreciation, experience sorrow, know joy, and are able to reach out to others. We may have adapted the beliefs of others, or been encouraged to create our own. The freedom or restrictedness of our experience can shape how deeply the word "God" or the word "Love" touches us. How much of our power have we given away? How much fear have we accepted? Have we had to grapple with asking ourselves, "How much of a sinner am I? Will I go to hell for not going to church and conforming?" On the other hand, have we opened to know deeply the feeling of love, the appreciation for the miracle of life, and of nature and all there is?

In our formative years, we may also have been exposed to fear-based doctrines and disciplines. Our relationship with the words "God" and "Love" may have become rooted in fear and hate. We have come into a period that will touch every soul and embrace the foundations of every religion, because it speaks to us all in the same language…the language of love. It is a language that we all understand, simply because we ARE love. This prophesized era and this glorious time is our grand opportunity to let go and let our collective, divine essence pervade.

It is our choice and power to forgive our parents and all who may have hurt us, realizing we are all doing the best we can with what we have. As we begin forgiving others and ourselves, we open ourselves to our truth and to an acceptance of the Divine Guidance. In this era, we are truly readied to embrace ourselves. Our true Selves are now emerging beyond the illusions and limitations of ourselves that we created in our childhoods. We are reminded of why we chose to come into this life. We can now blissfully realign with our soul memory.

A striking analogy found in the wild is that an entire community of male penguins will join together in a spiral to ensure newly laid eggs don't freeze while the females are out hunting. While the gale force minus fifty degrees Celsius (minus fifty-eight Fahrenheit) winds blow, the males huddle together, holding the eggs between their feet and rotate the spiral constantly, so as to equally share the warm center in the middle and the bitter cold on the outside perimeter of their circle. The same instinctive sentiment lies within us, because we are all united and connected; however, sadly, most fail to live in the vast Loving Universal Consciousness, as we have given away our power and relied heavily on our intellect. This has led us to put conditions on love, based on how we were loved and on our experiences with love.

Remembering our childhood experiences, we open to the awareness of entering a new period of relationships as well. As an example, only thirty years ago in North America, it was considered a major social disgrace to have a divorce, and the stigma still holds today in some communities and religions. Divorce rates are now at an all-time high. Realizing our own potentials, integrity, ideals, and spiritual awakenings, many of us have chosen not to remain in a marriage that no longer aligns and supports our spiritual awakenings. While this trend may have been a necessary adjustment, the curve is leveling off and we have now begun to align with our present partners and all those around us sharing The Knowingness and building ideals, thereby achieving more harmony in marriages and in the world and a decrease in the dramatic rate of divorces.[24]

---

[24] An eye-opening statistic is that more than 50% of students in a typical high school graduating class have parents who are divorced. According to a 2012 CBC News report, four in ten first marriages end in divorce. Source: alloneera.com/divorce

It is now our time to realize the reality of our illusion: we are not that which we think we are[25]. Our existence progresses far beyond the traits, circumstances, and constitution by which we insist on classifying ourselves as human beings on the three-dimensional plane. To come into our Knowingness and share it within every facet of our human lives, is to come into the power of becoming a true conduit of Spirit. We live collectively with one universal beating heart; we collectively open our Selves in alignment with "universal truth," instead of with our conceptual belief systems or the beliefs of others. **We are indeed each a universal vessel.**

As we live in the fifth-dimensional realm, we are far more loving, accepting, and unchallenging with our fellow beings at large and with those nearest to us. We come to forgive and release that which we once thought we were, in order to allow in the truths of whom we now know we are. The beginning of the awakening is to be able to look back at ourselves from the moment we are conceived and realize that who we are may be, in part, an illusion, built upon the so-called "facts" we share in common. We are composites of everything we knew growing up, and to become who we really are as Guided Beings, we simply let go of everything that does not align with our essence. Our essence is detached from our human selves and all the needs we perceive ourselves to have. The real "you" or "us" is one with the cosmic soul of the world. We are already one with all others, all Knowingness, and all love. Here is a wondrous accounting of The Thirteen Grandfathers.

The Thirteen Grandfathers

We speak to you as we are the Wisdom Keepers. We speak to you from the Lodge of Visions. We speak to you of this truth, the truth of your being, the truth of your life.

You do not have to make a choice as to where to focus your energy. You do not have to choose to serve others or serve yourself. You may simply now be aware that you are the center and you are the oneness. With this awareness comes peace. When people get confused their mind tells them that they have to make choices and that those choices limit the future and that those choices are

---

[25] See alloneera.com/sequoia

limited by the choices of their relatives and their ancestors, because in this way people send their mind in only one direction. It is a narrow path. It is a path that is very difficult because it is that path that tells you that every choice puts your energy in a direction of war or peace, vengeance or forgiveness, right or wrong. On that path, it is very difficult because by the nature of the flow of life is by nature, the flow of everything that is. There are moments on your journey when you move beyond a point of balance into a point of imbalance. That moment when you find yourself in a space of imbalance, you find that you have caused yourself pain and caused others pain and suffering. On this narrow path that we speak of, this path of right and wrong, there are responsibilities that you must carry as burdens and those are the stones that you carry on your back called guilt and shame and fear. This comes from thinking and the way that your relatives thought about good and evil and right or wrong. This comes from thinking that you are either right and you are here in a place that is acceptable or you are wrong and through being wrong you are condemned. It is a feeling of being wrong that takes people further out of balance because inside their hearts they lose the feeling and the knowledge and the truth of the center of their existence and that they are always in the flow of the universe.

They are always in the flow of the loving energy of Mother Earth. They are always the center and they are always totality. When a person thinks in a circle that circle is a Hoop of Life and when you live in a circle, there is no beginning and no end. In this place of balance, it is the way that your spirit moves in the world. It is the way of balance. When you live in a circle in this way knowing you are the center and you are the oneness, then it is easier to understand that the circle travels through many, many, many experiences, but is always moving back to itself. When you understand living in a circle, you understand that you cannot leave a place of love, because your life is always moving in a circle and you are always returning to those times of great joy. You are always moving in a pattern that returns you to balance. Even when you go through hard times and you are sorrowful because you are not separate from the times of joy when you live in a circle. You are at one with the times of joy and the times of sorrow. You are at one with the experience that every being has, because it is the nature of this world. When you think that you are walking in a path that is straight then that path can end. It can end at a point in the circle that is sorrowful and when that happens your spirit sometimes forgets how to flow in the rhythm of the circle and feels that that ending is all there is, that time of sorrow, that time of pain or that time when you have caused harm or suffering to others. But when you live in a circle you are always moving back to that place of love and spiraling into the center. Spiraling, always spiraling into the center, because there in the center there is balance. This is a circle teaching.

This teaching comes from the Lodge of the Grandfathers, from the Wisdom Keepers. We are the 13 Grandfathers. It is time now for us to speak. It is time for our wisdom to come to the people.

When you live in a circle, you know that all things are oneness. You are not separate from the most beautiful expression of the human soul and you are not separate from the most sorrowful. It is time now for the people all over Mother Earth to remember this teaching. A long time ago when people lived in the natural way, they lived with this rhythm. The rhythm was lost as you know they fought illness, confusion and depression because so many people on this Earth felt that their road ended at the place of sorrow and couldn't see the way that that circle would continue them to that place of love because they were on a path in a flow of Creator's Love, that sacred Hoop that we speak of. When we speak of the Mending of the Hoop, we speak of this knowledge and this awareness that the people who live on the Earth will begin to remember.

When we speak of this truth, we speak for a reason today. We are not speaking so that you can hear us. We are speaking so that our words can enter the world. We know the rhythm that is a wisdom that comes from knowing when to plant the seeds and when to harvest. We know and remember that when water flows from the Earth and you go to a spring to drink, there are times that the Earth will tell you she is bringing you a gift, a gift of healing, a gift to nourish your spirit. But if you think that all water is the same you are foolish. We know, we the Grandfathers know how to speak to the water. We know when to go to the spring for the gift of life. In our ancient memory, we knew how deep to plant the seed that the soil would protect it from dryness. We knew when to plant the seed and how long it would be until our relatives, the cloud people, would bring rain because we could talk to them. Because we knew the circle teaching that we speak to you of today. That is why there was a good harvest and that good harvest is what is important today to feed the hungry people. It is this gift that we speak of today that our voices enter the world that you live in, that we speak from the Lodge of the Wisdom Keepers. All of the beings, the spirit beings, that give you life. They are the ones that hear us today, the spirit beings of the water, the trees, the Earth, the spirit beings of life, because through this messenger today you can hear our words in a language that you understand in a way that touches your heart. But the speaking of these words at a sacred time on a sacred day of this deer dance, the speaking of these words is a gift from the Wisdom Keepers and it is heard by the elementals as you call them, by the nature spirits because they can hear our voice. You think that your language is so important. But the language of truth, the language of oneness, the language of the sacred message, when it is spoken in this way, it is heard by the living things that give you life. It enters your world as a sacred hoop of rhythm, a sacred hoop of life, a gift from Creator. When a message is given on a day like today and the trees can feel this message the Earth feels this message. As the birds awaken this morning and begin their song of the day, their song will carry this message. They will sing this message into the world. That is the difference in just speaking something and giving a gift from the Source of Great Wisdom. Remember this, my grandchildren; you will learn to speak from your heart from your source inside of you from your wisdom lodge. When you speak from this place of the sacred hoop from the wisdom lodge in your heart, you will learn the rhythm again. You will remember the rhythm again. You will remember this teaching and when you speak from this place of wisdom and peace you will remember how to speak in a way that the trees hear your voice and that the birds sing that song in the morning that carries the message to the world. A long time ago, this is what was meant by we could communicate to the animals. A long time ago, this is what was meant by we can communicate to the trees and to the Earth. This is the 1st teaching of the 13 Grandfathers.

Aho. We are blessed.

"When you speak from this place of the sacred hoop from the wisdom lodge in your heart, you will learn the rhythm again."
Judith K. Moore

We thank you, dearest Judith, for this refreshing reminder of our true essence. We all have tribal roots and our returning to speaking to the sacred fire and merging with the cycles of the moon and all of nature, is the blessing of our return to our balance in the "oneness circle." This vital message is the basis of the All One Era gatherings on the full and new moons in the pyramid and around the sacred fire.

Having made the conscious choice to let go of our illusions and preconceived notions of who we are, we are becoming one with the essence of all that is – the "I Am." It is at this choice we cast ourselves ahead on the path to fully opening our Selves into a joyous journey into the unlimited. We are no longer bound by that which we thought we were. We progress exponentially to now see the vastness of all that is, including our own individual truly grand potentials. In a fifth-dimension Guided life, there are endless possibilities…and perhaps one could say, **ONLY possibilities** in the circle of love.

~

Just before dawn after my death experience in the Kekuli, I awakened next to the smoldering embers of the fire and called to my sweet dog, Wolf Girl (half wolf, half dog). Slowly, we hiked all the way to the top of the mountain to greet the rising sun. Wolf Girl and I had climbed the mountain behind the vineyard many times before, but never in such dim pre- dawn light. It was an ambitious, clumsy endeavor, but she helped me so much by leading the way. Our timing was impeccable, as the moment we reached the summit, RAA (our star) broke over the horizon. I sank to my knees in awe, into the deepest and closest embrace of our oneness that I have ever reveled in.

The death experience brought home many realizations, including that we are not nothing and we are not small. We are vast like the entire universe! We created our bodies, and we created this splendid planet to behold the scenes of our majesty, our genius, and to live in glory with all there is. We are all one and therefore, individually, we are servants to the whole. Every day, we can stand in wonderment and exultation, seeing everything before us as the total union with our sun, our Earth, and our moon, the stars and our Selves. Today, so much of our energy is absorbed in computer/tv screens night and day, separating us from our natural connection. Perhaps now, more than ever, it is our time to surrender to Spirt and merge into our thrilling "God Selves" where "those beyond the sun" lay yearning to communicate with us!

> *"Every dream is reality as long as you believe it to be real.*
> *The one and only reality, the only objective reality there is,*
> *is the self: God!"*
> Elisabeth Haich, Initiation

Reflections

My dad used to brag that his youngest (of his three) brother, Bret Cipes[26], was a brilliant entertainer and could do tricks on stage. He could fan a deck of cards in front of an audience and call out the sequence. Once, when I was about nine, he put his hands on my shoulders, and looked me in the eyes and said, "<u>NEVER</u> speak against yourself! There are always people who will speak against you. Never say or think <u>anything</u> negative about yourself." His incredibly wise words have helped me many times, and I have reached out to many to never speak or think against themselves. I wonder if he knew then the prophetic full meaning of his words.

In March of 2000, I sponsored a young lady, named Davina, whom I'd never met, to join us on a leap of faith adventure. She was on dialysis and facing kidney failure. We visited the renowned psychic healer Joao de Deus, known as "John of God" in hopes that he could heal my new friend. We settled into our posada (inn) near Joao's rustic retreat in the most beautiful village up high in the lush green hills of Brazil, with distant views of the valleys below. The dark red earth there was teaming with quartz crystals, and guests immediately felt the exciting, yet calming, energy as they came through the gate of the sanctuary. It was so warm and inviting, like a homecoming: very intense and very peaceful at the same time.

---

[26] Bret Cipes was a Hollywood character actor and the co-author of the popular book *Will Hollywood Love You?*

A continuous fresh breeze kept us cool in the hot sun, as we were treated to the most heavenly-tasting freshly prepared meals consisting of freshly harvested produce grown in the red earth. We found ourselves surrounded by beautiful red-skinned people who walked barefoot and lived in tiny shacks, each with their own thriving garden. There were animals everywhere, and a sense of timelessness engulfed us. There were no supermarkets or banks, and very few motorized vehicles. Traveling was by foot or by mountain-equipped buses and tough little taxicabs that maneuvered their way through the muddy unpaved roads.

At an elevation of over three thousand feet, we were just above the rain forests and located precisely in an area well known for sightings of unidentified flying objects. When the night sky was clear, you could so clearly see the universe beyond planet Earth, as if seated in a planetarium. On the last evening of the retreat, and in a glorious mood from all that loving energy, I joyfully and jokingly invited our group of twenty of us who had travelled together to Brazil to step outside to see "The UFO!" They all came out to glance up at the clear sky in good fun. There was, of course, no UFO to be seen. Most of my new friends laughed at me and twelve of them went back inside the posada. This was when it happened! The remaining eight of us – Joyce, Frannie, Tisha, Lori-Jean, Auradais, Linzee, Davina, and myself, saw a triangle of three bright lights moving slowly across the sky. Then we saw the triangle make a sharp turn and move in the opposite direction, then stopping abruptly, and then moving slowly in an upward direction. We had no doubt that it was in fact a foreign movement of light! I immediately called for our twelve friends who had retreated back into the inn to join us once again, but, like the boy who cried wolf too many times, I was ignored by all but four of them.

The twelve of us then walked over to a field away from all electric light pollution, where we were immediately taken by what seemed to be the triangle playing a game of "hide and go seek" with us! At this point, Auradais took some deep breaths and invited us to join hands and stand in a circle. She then sent out an intention/prayer asking for protection, guidance, and permission to have the entities join us, and for us to be as one. We grounded ourselves and began toning. Beginning from the root chakra at the base of our spines, we could feel the energy rising all the way up through each of our chakras to the crown at the top of our heads, releasing the Kundalini Serpent. We chanted in unison as our energies rose up above our heads towards the foreign triangular light. At that point, their lights changed, and we knew that our final chants had raised our vibration to a state in which we were in harmony and at one with their frequency! It was quite an achievement and incredibly significant!

One of the women, Frannie, could feel the energy around us increasing immensely. Within minutes her voice began to change, taking on a very low deep burly tone like that of a man. She slipped into a trance-like state and began speaking to us in a very loud authoritative voice. We all jumped! That was when the entities then began sharing a number of messages with us through Frannie:

1. "Greetings Beloved ones. We are speaking to you through your person. Do you understand?"

We stood awestruck and in complete unison responded, "Yes!"

2. "We are always here and we have not been welcomed by the residents here for eons. We are very pleased that you have called upon us for communication. Do you understand?"

We all responded, "Yes!"

3. "We have called upon you. Remember that as you have called upon us, we have called upon you. It is our great delight. Do you understand?"

We all loudly responded, "Yes!"

4. "All of you will be like transmitters. Feel that part of your body where the connection is felt. Information packets have been disbursed throughout your body to be opened throughout your lives, beneficial to all of your respective friends, family, and community. Do you understand?"

We all confirmed and felt the area in our bodies where we chose to accept the gift of energy in our bodies.

5. "You and those who you come in contact with will feel this energy when you shake hands or hug, or consciously reach out. Feel (allow) these energies to flow through you to all you touch for all your lives. Do you understand?"

We joyously confirmed!

6. "This will allow them to come closer into this dimension."
7. "We will communicate with you on your levels of dimension, not as if we have physical bodies; we do not. We are not in form, we are energy. Understand?"

"Yes!"

8. "Our ships are about the size of this town; they are like whole cities." (Something about bringing their cities together with our cities was heard by Davina).
9. "We have many cities, as you do."
10. "Pay attention to your dreams tonight and always."
11. "Share the dreams."
12. "We, (our group) are the ones who will bring them (these other beings) closer to everyone in a loving way."
13. Auradias heard something about upping our frequency for all times.
14. "We are very grateful that you have chosen to open your receptiveness."

"We all agree and confirm!"

Auradais then asked the entities what form they took. Once again, they responded through Frannie, in the same slow, deep, male voice. They described themselves as being very tall (over seven feet) and referred to themselves as "light beings" – a term they believed we were familiar with. They explained their vibration was too high a frequency for the human eye to see. For this reason, they were invisible to us, but we would be able to see their silhouettes, as they were wearing capes. At that point, they invited us to come aboard their ship! They were indeed glowing light, and very tall with broad shoulders, which we could see by their capes. They had no mouths, just round human-shaped heads.

15. Their final messages through Frannie were repeats of their being very grateful.
16. "Speak from your hearts. Very important," they also shared.
17. "This communication is ended."

I wrote notes just after our encounter and invited several of us to recount the experience in their own handwriting. Kathy Bliss, a long-term assistant to a Bishop of the Catholic Church, was one of the last four to join us. She shared the experience in her own words:

"When I got there late, mid-channeling, we were gifted with implanted packets. These packets will unfold in the future as gifts – good things and blessings, which we are to share with family and all we meet (shaking hands/hugging). They will feel it. We were asked to identify the body part(s) where they were placed. It was obvious where that was. They were very grateful for our receptiveness and said not only were we calling to them, but they were calling to us as well. They talked about our paying attention to our inner levels, as they were giving us a tour of their ship. I could see from standing toward the outer circumference of their main chamber, looking down a ribbed hallway glowing with reddish-brown and purple-blue. Their speaking again brought me back into the logical mind to interpret their words. They said they 'lived' in villages of ships, or maybe we could think of them as cities, or even countries as we knew them.

"I got the feeling they were working on transitioning to a lower vibration in order to interact with us, just as we worked at raising our vibrations to connect with them. I also got the feeling there will come a time when they will be able to interact with mainstream Earth people, who will become more and more accustomed to their energy. This will be made possible because we were to be the

forerunner energies, interacting with other humans while we carry packets or gifts of energy from the entities, and share those with them. We now carry their energy for all time. It will be very helpful to us. We may begin to have interactive, informative dreams because of this experience beginning tonight. We will remember this experience as very integral to the remainder of our lives. This communication is ended."

Davina Huey also shared her account of boarding the ship:

"I saw the ribbed hallway and a large empty circular room. The color in the hallway was more a purple-grey strobe; there were different colored lights, kind of like the crystal room at Joao's clinic."

It is a prophecy that when the student is ready, the teacher will appear. In the practice of proactively opening and surrendering ourselves to be conduits of Spirit, we become both teachers and students. When our bodies are in this vibratory state, we not only ARE everyone there is, but we are nourished by them, and we can proactively nourish them. My constant awareness of our "Star Brethren" experience while visiting Joao de Deus has been a glorious gift. My vivid dreams, epiphanies and love are greatly enhanced as I am constantly in awareness of my responsibility and of my service. I continuously send my blessings of love to all I touch and to strangers as I pass through all my journeys. I send them now, with all my love and all my soul energy, to each and every one of the readers or listeners of the words in this book. For the first time since the boarding of the ship in March, 2000, I have chosen to reveal this extraordinary and fully credible experience of boarding the star-ship. I feel the complete absence of fear of reprisal or criticism in this new era of planet-wide ascension, with us welcoming the ever-present Loving Universal Consciousness, and I feel strongly that the time is now to accept all of our brethren in the entire Galactic Universe as one with us.

We are here to merge with unlimited creation, and with the nurturing of our Earth. We are ready to unite in gatherings, where we create an energy conducive to catapulting our realizations and co-create our rejuvenation, peace, harmony, abundance, and bliss. These universal truths and the Knowingness that surrounds us at all times (the LUC) are the keys to rescuing our Selves and our planet. Let's not throw our hands up in the air anymore. We are fully capable of effecting all there is. There are no more Knowing entities in the universe then we are; we are All One in the same Knowingness. The entities that welcomed us were simply vibrating in different consciousness dimensions which we are capable of receiving.

To cherish our physical Presence, while realizing we are not the physical, is to know that we are spiritual beings having a human experience. As we free our Selves from illusions, judgements and attachments, we are opening and becoming vessels of Divine Love, All One Forever Beings! Let's take back our power and save our grand creation...HEAVEN ON EARTH AWAITS US!

The Makwala Memorial Kekuli at
the Summerhill Pyramid Winery

*"Honoring moon cycles is how
First Nations people have
stayed in touch with nature,
and it is through this connection
that we develop a love of nature
and we learn how to love life,
so we don't go on wanting
for the rest of our lives.
Love of nature is love of life"*

Stephen Cipes
A quote from an interview with Wine Trails magazine, fall 2016

Chapter Six

THE END OF WANTING

It was difficult to call it a dream, as I felt so very much awake. Before me had appeared the clearest image of two huge rectangular metal spikes that seemed to float in the air, separated in the middle by a void. I could see the interrelation between the two huge metal pieces, watching them being pulled toward each other and then repelling, much like the actions of magnets. As I witnessed their unspoken communication, I could see these metallic forces as all encompassing, bringing to fruition the deepest wisdoms of all Knowingness. The beaming light of their connectedness was casting away what darkness lay in the void between the spikes. The unspoken understanding between them was clearly the demarking of an all-powerful center of intelligence.

Standing before those two massive spikes, all of our truth and all of our illusion was revealed and open to a shift. There was no uncertainty, fear or complexity, just a bearing of the naked truths of our presence. There was an extremely intense draw and need to bring the two powerful spikes together, after their having been cast as separate entities, spaces, and times for so long. Before me, the edges of the two spikes began to mesh, and then I saw it: the metal spikes were but representations of a draw so magnetic it could never be denied. One of them was all of us, as spiritual beings on this human plane, and the other, God or Spirit Supreme. It was a merging of two worlds so often seen as different polarities – one our human three-dimensional plane, and the other the spiritual fifth-dimensional and beyond realm. I could, with every cell of my being, feel those two metal pieces wanting to merge, and I knew that they were the solidified representation of us and of God Love, and of our connection to eternity.

I witnessed in awe, our auras merging with that of God Love, Divine Energy, and Angelic Light. The tiny edges of the once-distinct poles intertwined with each other as if dancing in a mystical vapor. They came together in such peace and harmony, yet with the magnitude of two freight trains meeting in the night. Within such a small space of "time," magnificence was revealed. Together as one with Divine Love, there was an overwhelming certainty that our multi-dimensionally Guided physical actions would lead to massive expansion! It was a sense of Knowingness so exhilarating, so magnificent, heavenly, and peaceful, even with the full awareness that we were going to have to work hard together now to make manifest what we know is possible. The purpose for the merging became everything. Where there once existed questions, or wanting, there now firmly stood certainty, a great triumph had been unveiled!

Emerging from that dream, I knew we must all savor our precious time. We can relieve ourselves of our illusions, and stand naked and unburdened in service in a life that is ours to create. I learned that to bring light to delusion and to bring an end to our human wanting is to wholly connect us to receivership of the love in the multi-dimensions, in both our waking and sleeping states. We sojourn in these bodies and we travel in them to far-reaching heights and to unlimited fathoms below. In the movement of our physical bodies and vastness of our dreams, our huge hearts can either plummet to the darkest depths or soar to lightest heights; the choice is ours.

In the midst of an early morning deep meditation, the question came through me of what it is that we want. The resonating response from within was that we all want so much, yet we need so little. The question inherently burning in all of us, no matter how materially well set or how needy we may be, is: What do we want for the good of the whole of humanity? Where is the comfort level we are all seeking and striving for? How do we attain the abundance we all know is here for us?

We have created a world facing utter destruction because we have selfishly chosen to focus on that which we personally desire. We have torn down forest upon forest to fulfill a desire to read glossy magazines and eat mass-produced foods. The resulting pollution from industries processing our precious natural resources have led to the threatening of the disappearance of ocean life and to the severe compromise of the purity of our drinking water and to the air we breathe. Industry has exponentially expanded to meet our perceived needs of material things, many of which may not be essential for our health or well-being. Huge economic resources have been invested to perpetually ready us for war, because we have believed peace is something we need to fight for. Perhaps what we really need is to step back a moment and count our blessings. Maybe we can do with a lot less and still maintain our comfort levels. These quotes have helped me put my life in perspective and more importantly, to become a being who yearns for us to all see our eternity and cherish it.

The Bhagavad Gita verse 18:12 and 18:20:

Krishna

18:12 When work is done for a reward, the work brings pleasure, or pain, or both, in its time; but when a man does work in Eternity, then Eternity is his reward.

18:20 When one sees Eternity in things that pass away and Infinity in finite things, then one has pure knowledge.

We have been born of the egg and sperm of a mother and father, and exist with a glandular system powered by the electrical energy flowing through our beating human hearts. Our bodies breathe collectively as parts of the whole. We share animalistic needs and a progression of life that flows through periods of both wellness and disease, giving and receiving. We are products of our upbringing and relationships, and we are continuously influenced by the economies and communities of which we are a part. We share the same basic needs for food, shelter, education, understanding, and love.

~

From where does our wanting originate? Our world, and the messaging and focus therein, are that which we have created. Through expectations and demands on ourselves and on everyone around us, we have created our human reality: one magnetic spike existing on its own, withdrawn from all other dimensions. We always bring ourselves back in alignment through the alleviation of judgment, paranoia, fear, vanity, greed, comparison, competition, and separation. Our miseries and the dire states of our Earth, stem from the denial of that which we truly are. To come to know our true essence is to realize a state of oneness with all of the Earth and all of the multiple dimensions. This state of "receivership" brings an end to our wanting and a coming home to that which we actually already are. We choose whether to bring together the proverbial magnetic spikes as one, or to leave between them a void, a space that creates a longing for more.

Organic veggie potluck and drumming and dancing in the Kekuli after a typical full moon gathering in the Pyramid. NOTE: Are they orbs or a camera phenomenon?

Knowingness or Consciousness can be thought of as "The Void," because there is the absence of matter. In a state of Knowingness, whether it is for a fleeting moment or at all times, it is like floating between where the stars and their planets revolve, or between where the neutrons and protons of atoms revolve. It is the resting place where our universe is created. It is the place from which we manifest matter. This void or empty space is the cosmic glue that unites us all. As we focus on the pituitary gland between our eyebrows in the center of our brains, and align our electrical-in-nature bodies in deep meditation, or when we are in dream states or have a jolt or a sudden epiphany, we are resonating with the Holy All-Oneness of Knowingness.

Suppose we were all to unplug all of our electronic devices, tone down the voices in our minds so strongly conditioned by society, momentarily cease worrying about money, and just step out into nature and surrender to a greater Knowingness. Could we then begin the process, the creation of a life no longer centered upon chasing after our whims and desires? Given space, could we balance and level out our relentless thirst, hunger, aggressiveness, need to win, and our ceaseless drive to earn money for material possessions? Perhaps we could realize that in a space filled with striving and wanting, we have kept ourselves from the simplicity of trusting, surrendering and opening to a boundless flow! Can we come to the realization that all we actually need is surrounding us and within reach at all times? Can we fully come into the Knowingness that we ARE all there is and welcome it with open arms?

While eating smoked salmon sushi in a tiny Japanese restaurant off Times Square in Manhattan before the matinee performance of Aladdin, Esther asked me the question: "Do we separate the soul from the body *before* we kill the fish or the animal so it's just the body?" After a brief pause, she went on to say, "We kiss the fish and hug the fish or the animal and then we kill it? Why we kill the fish?"

My answer: Because in nature, we are all interconnected. We live by and for each other – one whole living entity that includes all there is…however, when there are predators (killers), such as us human beings – smart, plentiful (eight billion of us), resourceful and ambitious (to always get ahead of each other) – nature suffers to the astonishing state of complete ruination! Let me draw you a graph, Esther, of the last ten thousand years of us humans living with all of the plants and animals on the earth, and of our generation of humans living with them. Look at that! There is one big long flat line with hardly any change in ten thousand years, and then, all of a sudden, a line straight up! What happened in the last hundred years to cause such a big change? Why have thousands of animals and plants and even original humans become extinct in such a short time, and why do they continue to become extinct every day? What is so different about the last hundred years? In a word, REVERENCE – Reverence for ourselves, Reverence for our collective Presence, Reverence for our Holy Oneness with all there is, Reverence for each other, and Reverence for our precious planet. This combined with the "industrial revolution" that put instruments of destruction in our hands as never before.

If we ARE all there is, there does not lie anything outside of us that could leave us wanting. All of the physical desires we are taught to want as a global society are put into perspective when paralleled with the true *needs* of The Soul of the World. The true sense of all there is does not lie in tangible objects or dollar signs, but rather in the energy, love, and pure potential that is within us. We all know intuitively that we can have it all! Material prosperity begins to flow when we are in harmony with ourselves and all there is! We can manifest true heaven on Earth; the choice is ours and the timing is highly conducive in this new glorious era!

At the age of eighteen, driven by my fierce need to be independent, I developed the goal of becoming a millionaire by the age of thirty and ceaselessly worked with every encounter focused on building my wealth. I truly had a silver tongue, speaking only to make money. By the time I was twenty-one, I had singlehandedly sold out an entire subdivision as a real estate broker, began investing in large tracts of land, and built a lakefront house and filled up the driveway with two Cadillacs. In spite of a relentless inner urge to follow my heart and not my head, I relentlessly forged on with my goal to become a millionaire, beating my target at age twenty-seven! It was then, through a series of circuitous circumstances, which included some major life changes, that I was led to embrace a profound seven-day "short death" Kundalini Yoga Meditation experience. This was the turning point that allowed me to return to my greatest teacher: Myself.

For seven days, I sat in stillness in the lotus position, in deep Samadhi, the heavenly state of Nirvana, without eating or sleeping. It was during these deepest of meditations that I had my most life-changing revelations. I realized my "heart Self" and became one with it. I decided to not use my silver tongue solely to make money anymore. I decided not to speak unless my words were a direct expression of my heart. After the seventh day and a blissful sleep, I placed a small smooth stone under my tongue and kept silent for more than three weeks, gradually returning to normal speaking as I simultaneously gifted all of my material possessions to friends and family. This cleansing experience empowered me so greatly, as it has blessed me with the perspective of being able to be detached from material possessions, and more importantly, from illusions and delusions about life.

I will never forget that morning of the seventh day of meditation sitting in the lotus position. I had asked Annie to please give us the daily reading from our Guru in India. It was February 29th, a leap year, and there was no prepared quote for the day. I asked her to please phone India, and sure enough, she was able to reach our guru directly. This day his quote was: *"Earth is test, heaven is rest."* In that moment, I felt as though I had passed an extraordinary test. I felt as though I had discovered a grander family. I was in oneness with all, and in harmony with my Self, the entire cosmic dimensions of all there is. I had allowed myself to be a receiving conduit, a living vessel of and for all the love in the universe!

Now that we've all explored and completely delved into every other type of diversion, folly, elixir, and thrill, and every type of situation dollars and human ingenuity could ever possibly imagine and invent, we can now settle down and let it all go! Our peace and the end of our wanting centers in our surrender to the Wholeness of Consciousness, or God, Allah, Buddha, Brahma, Jesus, Christ Energy, Love, Higher Self, Spirit Supreme, or however we choose to term that which is undeniably Divine and infinitely who we are. When we no longer give away our lives by being focused on wanting and doing, and pleasing, impressing, or stealing from others, grand love freely flows through us.

During a recent pre-dawn meditation, while sitting in lotus position, a question came through me: *What is it you want?* I then experienced a significant jolt. A leap of faith rushed through every vein and space of my being. It was a charge that caused me to immediately jump up. Arising, I went outside, barefoot, in the dark winter stillness and walked down to the beach, where the waves were gently lapping on the shore and the magnificent waning moon was shining brightly reflecting her light upon the water. With every ounce of my Being, I bellowed out loudly, *From the Lord God of my being, indeed! Unto the Lord God of all of creation, indeed! I set forth that we all now BE in the age of receiving!* I knew instantly that the jolt would be felt, heard, smelled, tasted, and rejoiced in that all-powerful moment, and that we <u>ARE</u> one with this deserved precious paradise of our Earthly home in a splendid eternal universe! THIS is all we want! It is our precious, deserved heritage where we share one heart, one home, one love. My prayer is for all humanity to now rise to the occasion in consciousness and allow our self-realization to bloom.

Ms. Lindsay McLellan, aka "Infinity," a continuously-barefoot, free spirit, twenty-one-year-old sums up these sentiments beautifully in her poem, "The Spaces Between Space."

The Spaces Between Space

We were just a bunch of children, Playing our
games in the pre-dawn of our lives.
Night and day were one,
And we sang and danced through eternity, as the stars turned and were born overhead. Dark
forests held magic that called to us: Endless oceans drowned us in power.
We felt as one...We dreamed as one.
We didn't know the difference between reality and fantasy,
But we knew there was no right or wrong.
We lived for the moment, Learning the name
of each action we took.
Forces that loomed on the sidelines died quietly,
As we had no fear to feed them.

The light that embraced us was ignored,
As we could only live simply, From one breath to the next.
And just as lessons learned from living are gold beyond the veil,
The knowledge hidden here was long
kept too far within to grasp.
And so we were,
Beings in the spaces between space,
Without comprehension of existence,
And we grew in brilliance
Until we once more became everything.

Lindsay's silky poem reminds us we are co-creating in every moment and always have been, simply by being one with our unlimited loving Selves. This wisdom can be achieved at any chronological age, especially as we return to our spontaneous ever-joyful little girl or little boy Selves. We have the ability to dream anything and do anything, and to go to any extremes, or we can chase endless goals and acquire endless possessions. The choice is ours. Merging in the Now, all we "want" is that which serves the greatest good for all, for we become one with all. We go from self-centered egotists blind to the consequences of our greed to being ambassadors of abundance for all. More importantly, we realize that whatever we want manifests itself. We ARE the Masters!

At this time in our time, maybe we all need to step back, take some deep breaths, and go within to our hearts, our soul memories, our essence, and our Knowingness. I call it connecting with the ever-present Loving Universal Consciousness; you can call it intuition, or anything that feels right. We know, "We can't change anyone else, we can only change ourselves." The time is NOW to begin to gather around the sacred fire on the full and new moons and re-connect with nature and each other *before* we kill the fish that Esther so lovingly was concerned about.

Excerpts from the ancient Bhagavad Gita, edited by Juan Mascaró, give us a glimpse of the supreme state of being. In verses 15:14, 15:15, 15:16, 15:17, 15:18, 15:19 and 15:20, Lord Krishna speaks to Arjuna, his subject;

117

Krishna

15:14 I become the fire of life that is in all things that breathe; and in union with the breath that flows in and flows out I burn the four kinds of food.

15:15 And I am in the heart of all. With me come memory and wisdom, and without me they depart. I am the knower and the knowledge of the Vedas, and the creator of their end, the Vedanta.

15:16 There are two spirits in this universe, the perishable and the imperishable. The perishable is all things in creation. The imperishable is that which moves not.

15:17 But the highest spirit is another: it is called the Spirit Supreme. He is the God of Eternity who pervading all sustains all.

15:18 Because I am beyond the perishable, and even beyond the imperishable, in this world and in the Vedas, I am known as the Spirit Supreme.

15:19 He who with a clear vision sees me as the Spirit Supreme he knows all there is to be known, and he adores me with all his soul.

15:20 I have revealed to thee the most secret doctrine, Arjuna. He who sees it has seen light, and his task in this world is done.

One of the most memorable sentiments I've heard repeated by those who have survived near-death experiences is, "Upon my 'death bed,' I realized I wasted ninety-nine percent of my life on all the many petty things that have little or no importance!" At the key moment of our transition, we may have huge regrets that we did not devote more than a tiny fraction of our lives to our original sublime soul intentions. We may carry guilt for hiding our intentions only to conform or in order to be accepted by society and our peers. We are instantly forgiven as there is always only the NOW. The Divine, non-conditional, angelic, loving NOW. In the aggressive masculine-energy-driven technological era from which we are just emerging, we have been giving away our power in unprecedented proportion. We have been focusing upon gratification of wanting, and upon relying on and feeding off others for our choices and direction. Now, halleluiah, we see that as receivers, we quickly lose patience for the old paradigm of the human drama and the patterns of merciless aggression. Our sense of urgency shifts from human accumulation to the expansion of consciousness, of rescuing ourselves and in turn our planet. This colossal shift to our receiving state nurtures our own natural instincts and purpose to be one with our Mother Earth and all the universe, and allows us to trust that we have internally-focused access to all that we need. There is no separation, no need for distinction through wanting more and more possessions or titles; there is already splendor and grandness within each and every one of us! The expansion of our consciousness and end to our wanting is the answer to naturally easing our relentless demands, polluting and destroying our planet, and replacing it all with a soul-centered desire to treat *her* and ourselves with utmost nurturing compassion. The only avenue then becomes listening to our Guidance, and following our true purpose of Self-Realization and of nurturing and supporting our Selves and Earth. We have everything we need now to thrive, individually, collectively, and as one with our planet. We are one with The Soul of the World, the center of everything we need and love. The wanting of contrived happiness will never save our planet; our expansion of loving consciousness will.

The truth is that all of us jump into this life with a Grand Purpose, which becomes either watered down or forgotten, as we face the challenges of living. However, many of us carry our original intention strongly and are natural leaders in restoring the magnificence of our own and the collective intention. The blessing is that our purpose is brought to light by opening to the fifth-dimensional consciousness we are all a part of. Our ability to be open to this state of being sparks our creativity like no other. We join a world of endless, boundless potentials and co-creativity.

We have at our fingertips, the ability to instantly realize all there is. With a shift in consciousness, we can see, enjoy, be, relish in, and co-create it ALL. When we come to be in that moment, we gain wonderment in all that we already have within us and in our lives to be appreciated without attachment or longing, and we return to our truth and purpose in this life. In our acknowledgement of the Loving Universal Consciousness flowing through us, we know that we are not defined by that which we see or have. We are at home in our Original Splendid Intention as conduits of all of creation. To live in such a heavenly state is to fully realize our dream of Being at peace with our Selves and with all others. We take back our power and experience the true thrill of being alive! We free ourselves to realize such a state once we can clearly see that we are not just these bodies or just this Earth spinning around, but rather, eternal, loving Beings, all connected as one.

Stephen and Esther in Central Park, NYC.
Photograph by Joel Cipes.
"Do we separate the soul from the body before we
kill the fish or the animal so it's just the body?"

*Left to Right: Ezra Cipes, Rio Branner (Cipes), Ruth Cipes,
Dr. Jane Goodall, Stephen Cipes, and Gabe Cipes
in Kelowna, BC Canada April 2017.*

"Those who are in tune with God
can change men's hearts."
"Remain calm, serene[27] , always in command of yourself. You will
then find out how easy it is to get along."

Paramahansa Yogananda,1893-1952
Author of Autobiography of a Yogi
and founder of The Self-Realization Fellowship.

---

[27] See alloneera.com/serenity

Chapter Seven

CREATING A PORTAL FOR PURITY

"Open your eyes and see me in all my splendor,
as I see you in all your splendor."
Mother Earth

One of the main reasons we created our physical existence is to evolve spiritually. In bodies, we experience physical changes first-hand. When in our ethereal bodies, we retain the memory of the sensations and the wisdoms and growth we nourished our souls with while in the physical. Our experiences while in our bodies last forever, as they become a part of our souls. We are now merging all the dimensions into our existence by willing it and creating within us portals for purity that allow the ongoing stream of love to abundantly flow through our bodies.

One very early, dark, star-studded morning in January, I awoke still half in a dream state, but full of the excitement of being alive. I stepped outside barefoot[28]. I grounded myself in the deep snow. Releasing the shock of the cold, a feeling of deep satisfaction overcame me as I merged with the "no time" and all there is. I felt with every atom in my cells, the Earth yearning for me to come and be one with *her*. She felt and acknowledged my presence! She feels and acknowledges our Presence! She blossoms and heals when we are sharing our excitement to be alive with her. She is us – our

---

[28] Video on grounding by Laura Koniver, MD: alloneera.com/grounding

bodies, minds, hearts, emotions, and totality of Spirit – and she lives through us, with us, and by us. That which we are, she is too, in an ever ebbing and flowing sea of masterful giving and receiving of her energetic tides.

The deterioration, destruction, ruination, and despair occurring within and all over our Mother cries out for us to share our light of love. The Spirit's gift is that we are her conduits of light and love! We were here when eternity began. Our deepest soul memory is as Light Beings, where we co-created the planet and animal kingdom and established our physical bodies on this plane. We did so to fully experience, nurture, and grow our Original Splendid Intention of an ever-expanding Loving Universal Consciousness, both physical and spiritual. We are the original entities, one with ascension consciousness in this time of times. Our Knowingness and our purity of intention are now bringing breakthrough blessings for all, as perhaps never before in these pivotal days in our times.

If we are to allow the source of universal love to flow into our union with the Earth and all therein, we revive within ourselves a comfort zone or a portal for *God Love* to flow. Through our Selves, we can begin to channel the greatness of pure love and light. Our lofty essence has been stifled by the experiences we have been subjected to by our parents, society, and all whom we meet because we have all been reduced to a highly restricted three-dimensional experience. Are we going to allow our preoccupation with the admittedly fiercely addictive human drama to continue to lead us into possibly facing the potential of absolute utter destruction? Are we truly unworthy of taking back our rightful power and glory? I am sure we are not! As we return to our all-Knowing genius Selves, we ascend to our metaphorical mountaintop, where we can clearly see how the human drama has stolen our lofty heritage and how it has so greatly restricted our rightful ascension, our return to our Grand Selves. We all have a genius-level knowingness that we own, that is a part of us. While subliminal, the Master within us is all there, within all of us, as part of our DNA.

The beauty of the All One Era, which we are collectively ascending into, is the acknowledgement of being multi-dimensional beings. We are now allowing the Angels to live through us, and fantasy and joy to return – a return to our little girl or little boy Selves, and our "thrilled to be alive" Selves! As we imagine and capture the fifth dimension, our all-loving home, we are instantly connected as

Forever Beings. Multi-dimensional awareness is so vastly different from that of the limited third-dimension awareness. The leap into it is unlabored and happens within a flash, a nanosecond, a snap of the fingers! The realization of such a state can often bring about a shudder or a jolt in our bodies. When we get this jolt, it is always a very positive sign. This jolt not only verifies that the message has registered, but also is "felt" universally by all of us!

The dawning of this era also represents motherly love merging with fatherly love – a grand balance. As we come forth in opening our Selves in our feminine receivership and unconditional love (the X chromosome), we also welcome in fatherly love – the love of all that is, with a yearning to have it flourish and expand in every way. We are collectively turning our attention to our newfound awareness that we are co-creating a genius level population. We have arrived in an ever-flowing divine love, where our most sacred prayers are answered. This is when we know our Selves and the truth of our Holy divinity and grand purpose.

In the year 1973, when Mathew David and I were a happy family of two, I had a vision of a World Peace Day. I chose his birthday, September 24th, to be a day of worldwide cessation of all business and communication – one day a year of silence, reverence for creation, and contemplation – a total planet-wide Sabbath. I wrote a letter to then-leader of the United Nations, Dag Hammarskjold, suggesting that the United Nations proclaim a World Peace Day. I sent copies to many for support, including a copy to Rabbi David Golovensky, who had been my Rabbi at my bar mitzvah in 1957. Rabbi phoned me immediately and invited me to come to his office. In awe of the opportunity, I drove to New Rochelle, New York and sat before this wise, white-haired, gentle man in his bookshelf-lined office. He asked me one question: "How are you Stephen? How is your home life?"

I then revealed how happy the two of us were and how beautiful it was to enjoy being both a mother and a father to a joyful and always happy little boy. I told him how Annie, the mother of our child, had decided to move to India to be with our guru, and how she had signed the legal papers to allow me to have sole custody of our son. He then said, "Stephen, achieving peace in the world is the easy way. Achieving peace in yourself and in your family, is the hard way." His words were profound. We all have to achieve peace within ourselves first and foremost, before we can extend ourselves to the whole. Rabbi helped me immeasurably in keeping my feet on the ground while I reach for the moon, the sun, and the stars in my heart. Interestingly, the celebration of International World Peace Day is now established worldwide and observed on September 21st of each year!

What a privilege and exalting experience it is to be alive in a body! Every day, we learn so much from our physical interactions. I have learned that becoming Realized Beings or Conduits of Spirit comes in the snap of the fingers. It can begin through countless mediums, teachers, experiences, and circumstances that further open our physical and mental Selves. Sacred geometry, yoga, meditation, group meditation, ceremony, sacred fires in ancient traditional structures, being one with nature, clean air, water, and food, and peaceful living are all very powerful; as is reserving a comfortable place that is private and quiet, neither too hot nor cold, either inside or outdoors, where complete seclusion can be gained. It is a space in which we are free to scream, chant, laugh, and sigh with as little interruption or distraction as possible. Seated on a chair or on the ground, cross-legged or in lotus position, we proactively create, with our physical bodies, a splendid space of oneness and complete openness. Turning our attention to hearing the sound around us, we focus on our breath and the light we see pulsing through our pituitary gland, also known as our third eye, between our eyebrows. Listening, breathing, surrendering, and focusing becomes the gateway to our receivership of Divine Guidance.

The first step in realizing purity and ascension is to recall that we indeed are love, and that the essence of the words "God" and "love" are synonymous. I find that meditation or just quietly sitting brings clarity and an overwhelming rush of our Holy Oneness with all there is. While focusing on our breath, we stretch and turn as much as our body allows. One can follow prescribed yoga exercises or simply move each part of our bodies to its limits. Feeling lighter and more open, we can then bend forward until our heads touch down between the knees, as we hold our breath and allow a tingling sensation and welcome an atmosphere where the surrounding Knowingness Vibrations can lower themselves as we raise ours, and we meet in the middle. The longer held, the grander the interaction with Spirit. This welcoming also is realized through powerful exhalation, one that encompasses a total-body pushing out of all of the air within, as in giving birth. Through our breath, we seat our all-Knowingness into our nervous system, brain, and every cell of our body, as it travels up through our spinal column to our medulla oblongata. Once centered in our breath, we bring our intention, with closed eyes, to the space between our eyebrows (our pituitary gland or third eye). This is the opening of all of the dimensions – a portal of unlimited consciousness and love. You may perhaps feel a jolt when you see yourself as a Realized Being. There, you also instantly see that we are *all* Realized Beings. As we each grasp hold of this simple yet profound truth, we see it can be achieved in a split second in this lifetime, in a body and at any age! We also clearly see that making this conscious decision to realize fifth-dimensional love allows us the incredible opportunity to manifest our most fervent intentions AND to achieve personal peace, abundance, and fulfillment! It is here that our Receiving Selves have opened the doorway to return home. We lose all aggression, competition, thoughts of material gain, and judgment when we surrender our ego-selves and merge with all there is. We come into full recognition that we are not ourselves and not our bodies, and lose our sense of me, instantly becoming one with all. This is a way to experience the Divine State of fifth-dimensional love. Actually, there are many other ways and there is no-thing we have to do. We only have to BE.

A beautiful excerpt from *The Hermetica: The Lost Wisdom of the Pharaohs* says it well:

The Initiation of Hermes

My senses were suspended in mystic sleep not a weary, full-fed drowsiness,
but an alert and conscious emptiness.
Released from my body, I flew with my thoughts,
and while I soared, it seemed to me,
a vast and boundless Being called my name:
'Hermes, what are you looking for?'

'Who are you?' I asked.

'I am the Way-Guide, the Supreme Mind, the thoughts of Atum the One-God.

CREATING A PORTAL FOR PURITY

I am with you always and everywhere.
I know your desires.
Make your questions conscious, and they will be answered.'

'Show me the nature of Reality. Bless me with Knowledge of Atum,' I begged.

Suddenly everything changed before me. Reality was opened out in a moment.
I saw the boundless view.
All became dissolved in Light united within one joyous Love.
Yet the Light cast a shadow, grim and terrible, which, passing downwards,
became like restless water,
chaotically tossing forth spume like smoke.
And I heard an unspeakable lament an inarticulate cry of separation.

The Light then uttered a Word, which calmed the chaotic waters.

My Guide asked:
'Do you understand the secrets of this vision?
I am that Light—the Mind of God, which exists before the chaotic dark waters of potentiality. My
calming Word is the Son of God the idea of beautiful order;
the harmony of all things with all things, Primal Mind is parent of the Word,
just as, in your own experience, your human mind gives birth to speech.

They cannot be divided, one from the other, for life is the union of Mind and Word. Now, fix your
attention upon the Light, and become One with it.'
When he had said this, he looked into me, I to I,
until, trembling, I saw in thought limitless power within the Light,
to for man infinite yet ordered world and I was amazed.

I saw the darkness of the deep, chaotic water without form

permeated with a subtle intelligent breath of Divine power.
Atum's Word fell on the fertile waters making them pregnant with all forms. Ordered by the
harmony of the Word, the four elements came into being,
combining to create the brood of living creatures.
The fiery element was articulated as the constellations of the stars,
and the gods of the seven heavenly bodies, revolving forever in celestial circles.
The Word then leapt up from the elements of nature
and reunited with Mind of Maker, leaving mere matter devoid of intelligence.

My Guide said:
'You have perceived the boundless primal idea,
which is before the beginning.
By Atum's will, the elements of nature were born as reflections of this primal thought in the
waters of potentiality. These are the primary things; the prior things;
the first principles of all in the universe.
Atum's Word is the creative idea the supreme limitless power
which nurtures and provides for all the things
that through it are created.

I have shown you everything why do you wait?
Write the wisdom you have understood in hieroglyphic characters,
carved on stone in the holy sanctuary.
Make yourself a spiritual guide
to those worthy of the gift of Knowledge, so that, through you,
Atum may save humankind.'

I was overwhelmed with gratitude to the All-Father who had graced me with the supreme vision.
In awe and reverence, I prayed, 'Please never let me fall away
from this Knowledge of your Being, so that I may enlighten
those who are in darkness.'

Then, with his power in me, I began to speak.

The aloof laughter at my words, but others knelt at my feet.
I told them to stand
and received the seeds of wisdom, which I will sow in you
with these teachings. So, listen, men of clay.
If you do not pay keen attention, my words will fly past you,
and wing their way back to the source from which they come.

Once we exist in the dimensions of love, we exist forever in the dimensions of love. We stay there at all times, even when eating, driving, relating, and talking. "Love never dies." The pulsating beat of our third eye is awakened and eternally open and beating. Our health and youth blossom and we become ageless, child-like, spontaneous, and in the moment. We are able to take on far more challenges and responsibilities than ever before, while remaining fully grounded. There are scientific studies on the profound hormonal changes individuals who are spiritually advanced have – they appear noticeably less aged at all ages, show their child-like spontaneity and joy and their Presence is felt, even in a crowded room.

Tuning into and becoming one with all of our spiritual dimensions is allowing in our Grand Selves, or the Master within us, on every level! Our bodies are the portals and channels of multi-dimensional love. We can help to achieve this extreme vitality by incorporating some or all of the following physical guidelines:

1. Striving to be as fully hydrated as possible, at all times, and with the healthiest of liquids and purest of water.

2. Ingesting only chemical-free and karma-free, organic or wild foods and beverages, which automatically contain the essence of love in highest vibrating form. Some may consider becoming a vegetarian or even eliminating all animal protein from their diet and embracing a

total plant-based, vegan diet. A vegan diet gives us the nourishment our bodies crave and need to rise to meet the vibration of Spirit. While this may seem like a severe departure and a daunting alternative, there are vegan recipes that rival the most gourmet animal protein dishes![29]

3. Staying physically fit with daily cardiovascular exercise keyed to and designed for our age, weight, sex, and physical strength.

4. Connecting with the Earth outdoors, feeling *her* Presence with our bare feet and bare hands in the earth. Communicating with *The Enchantress*, our moon, and with RAA, our glorious star[30] , making eye and body contact daily and in ever-increasing amounts.

There are several awesome ways to re-establish our connection with the Earth, even in the center of a big city! One very effective way is to put our bare hands and feet, and even our entire bodies, directly onto the Earth, allowing the Earth's natural electromagnetic energy to flow through us. We can reconnect, instantly recharging our silver cord electrical connections to all there is! Standing for just a few seconds in snow is a thrilling cleansing. Just the proactive Presence of our standing and touching and feeling and acknowledging oneness with our Earth creates a vibrancy that is felt in every atom of our respective beings.

We are electrical beings vibrating at 7.83 Hz. By removing ourselves as much as possible from technological screens such as cellular phones and any wireless tools, which all emit low-frequency radiation and vibrate (and invade us) at 60hz, we greatly enhance our all-one communication with each other and with nature. While we have developed remarkable instruments for astounding three-dimensional communication, our natural lines of natural direct communication between each other and with Spirit are vastly stifled. In addition, major illnesses such as cancer are now traced to over exposure to all forms of EMFs. I

---

[29] See Dr. Esselstyn's *Prevent and Reverse Heart Disease* diet and cook book and *The China Study*, showing how almost no cancer, heart disease or diabetes exists in huge populations where plant-based foods are prevalent!

[30] Sun Gazing: alloneera.com/sungazing

cringe every time I see a mother using a cellphone near her children, or a pregnant woman with a cellphone touching her body.

5. Breathing every breath of air with conscious intention, while listening to and enjoying stillness and quietness in its fullest. Dolphins and whales have one eye open at all times and are always practicing conscious breathing, as they do not have the auto-breath reflex in their brains that we and other animals have! Perhaps our mammals of the sea are our totally ascended brethren, and should be protected and embraced way more diligently.

6. Proactively maintaining full awareness of our bodies in everything we do. Always consciously listening to and living for ourselves as conduits of and for Spirit.

7. Living in the joyous spontaneity of our inner child, always in the now and in the Knowingness, that surrounds us and is us.

8. Returning to our ancestral tribal heritage by regularly participating in group meditation, music, chanting, drumming, dancing, ceremony, and feasting, all in honor of our immersion of oneness with nature and all there is.

9. Creating and manifesting intentions that carry the essence of a new paradigm for zero tolerance for chaos, arrogance, aggression, war, male dominance, and the constant striving for greed and control.

With purification of Self, our purpose is revealed, and we start to grow exponentially. We take charge of our heretofore misdirected mental energy and open it to our vast capability to literally know all there is to know, without limitation! We begin to celebrate our collective strength of purpose, our perpetuity and sustainability, our continuance and survival, not only as humans in bodies, but for all of nature – our trees, our whales, our dolphins, our elephants, our butterflies, our Earth, and her mountains, lakes, oceans, and skies. To be one with such revelations and to feel the original thrill of being alive within every cell of our bodies is to be in tune with our joyous love of life, our little boy or little girl Selves! It is a renewal of our original exuberance of being alive in a natural state, unaltered by pollution, addiction, fear, or societally-imposed regulations.

To open as receivers to the flow of multi-dimensional Knowingness, where our Presence is felt and the Presence of the Masters is felt, is to come into "God Realization," and to know that we are all Masters, reaching out to touch others. We are now receiving answered prayer; we are a Sea of Masters! As we harmonize with our souls and enrich our bodies, we are in fact enriching the entire world. It is a strengthening of the silver cord – our vertical connection between our Earthly three-dimensional plane and our multi-dimensional spiritual realms. We can clearly see now that by maintaining the intensity, vibration, and strength we have within, we stay connected to our all-Knowingness and are easily able to raise our Selves to feel and know our awesome oneness with all there is! **This is how we save our planet!**

Elessence, the Nature Spirit, herself.
Photo credit: Aaron DeSilva
alloneera.com/elessence.

"The self is life and the only reality, and whoever is initiated into the self – and in this way has come to know himself completely – loves everything and everyone equally, for he is one with them."

Elisabeth Haich

Chapter Eight

PLANET-WIDE ASCENSION

In 1985 in Bedford, New York, while swimming hard in my early morning exercise, I was gifted with a jolt of profound significance. In that moment, I beheld a vision of a planet-wide ascension[31]…one that would come naturally as we build a model of man and nature, a showplace of the majesty of nature and how we are *her* forever co-venturers. I jumped out of the pool and immediately remembered a recent conversation with our friend Mary from Scotland who raved about the fruit growing magical Okanagan Valley in British Columbia, Canada. I've always felt drawn to Canada as it was the birthplace of my beloved maternal grandmother, Esther and I'd always wanted to grow grapes! I left the very next day to explore finding the site in my vision!

I soon found the magnificent Summerhill Vineyard with its expansive vistas for miles up and down pristine Lake Okanagan in its glorious wilderness vortex of mountains and lakes. I immediately reflected on my vivid memory of a vision I had while on a visit to Thailand's Buddhist sanctuaries. One starry night I had slipped into stillness, awed by the magnificence of the Holy Buddhist sanctuaries and the vast universe above. In this stillness, I experienced a waking dream state and in that dream state, with my own hands, I constructed a pyramid of Divine proportion through a formula gifted to me. So bright and glorious was the structure that it was not possible to look at it without its shining light blinding my eyes. It was sacred in its geometry, and it was

---

[31] See alloneera.com/planetwideascension

awesomely powerful. Standing within the pyramid, I found myself surrounded by entities, both of this human dimension and of spiritual realms beyond. It was a Holy shrine, welcoming the presence of entities that arrived ethereally whenever they were called upon. I felt so thrilled and honored to be in the company of these spirits and they with me! I felt the intensity and vast importance of our rendezvous! The true sensation of awe and excitement did not leave me, and I knew that this vision must be preserved and honored and that it must become a physical reality. I felt exhilarated, in spite of the daunting nature of accepting such an assignment. This was the way! I would build a sacred structure, one that would provide a forum for the grand teachings that we are all one. This was my calling!

In 1986, we purchased the magnificent Summerhill Vineyard; and in 1987, our family of my wife Wendy and our four young boys moved into the vineyard house. I found myself loving working in the vineyard, getting my hands dirty changing the oil on the tractors, and enjoying the meditative state that comes with the intensive hours of tedious tractoring. However, I was aghast when the vineyard manager, Alan Porter, told me to suit up and put on a mask because we would be spraying Gramoxone on the vineyard that day[32]. I did it, but soon afterwards checked out the properties of Gramoxone and realized that it was one of the most toxic chemicals you could put on the planet and that it would no doubt be seeping into the lake which was our drinking water. I also feared the effects of the chemicals on my four little boys as I knew there was a correlation between chemicals and cancer in young children. Today there is an epidemic of cancer in children living next to vineyards in France[33]. I soon stopped using all chemicals and applied for organic status, which at that time was a seven-year ordeal. Through this process, I met a wonderful fellow Vineyard Manager, named Kenn Visser, who supported me on my vision to go organic and who encouraged me to contact the proprietor, Jack Davies, and his famous winemaker Alan Tensure of Shramsberg Winery in Calistoga, Napa Valley. Kenn brought them up to me and we expounded on the ideal growing conditions for making sparkling wine in the northernmost desert viticulture region in the world, where the intense flavor of the base cuvée would endure the second fermentation in the bottle.

---

[32] See alloneera.com/gramoxone

[33] Today there is an epidemic of cancer in children living next to vineyards in France. See the touching video at alloneera.com/epidemic

"Steve, you're wasting your time growing table wine. These growing conditions are magnificent for growing intensely flavored grapes for sparkling wine. They have probably the best combination in the world with the long, hot sunny days, being so North, your lack of rainfall, and your pristine air and water." I thanked them all and knew immediately that I had an amazing opportunity before me to bring pride to all Canadians by making the best sparkling wine in the world. I immediately set out to find a winemaker who had experience with sparkling wine and was introduced to Eric von Krosigk, who had been studying for eight years in Geisenheim, Germany making sparkling wine, but who had grown up in the Okanagan Valley! I flew to meet him in Germany and we hit it off amazingly. We immediately shared this great dream to bring the intense flavor of the grapes grown in our Okanagan Valley to the world. We then toured the sparkling wine regions of Europe including Germany with their famous Riesling Sekt and of course, Champagne, France. During that tour, I experienced a tingling in my hands whenever we would go into one of the many miles of underground Roman Arch cellars[34]. I asked why this was so and answered my own question when I realized that the Roman Arch was one of the three major shapes (the Roman Arch, the dome and the pyramid) that was automatically a sacred geometry chamber. The base cuvée, after it went through the second fermentation in the bottle, was then dosaged with a sweet reserve and placed in these Roman Arch cellars for a minimum of thirty days, for what they call the "marriage period," before placing the bottles on the shelves for sale.

I immediately decided to build a sacred geometry chamber at Summerhill to energize our uniquely spectacular wine during the marriage period! In 1988, Eric and I became co-founders of Summerhill Pyramid Winery and he joined me in British Columbia, where we replanted much of the vineyard with "Champagne clones" from France (Chardonnay, Pinot Noir, and Pinot Meunier) which really complemented our existing Geisenheim 21b clone Riesling. The first Summerhill Pyramid cellar was enthusiastically created to precision alignment and design to energize the wines. It was a thirty-foot square, one-and-a-half story, wooden frame pyramid with an indented concrete cellar. We then produced the first Cipes Brut, with a Riesling-based cuvee which was released in 1991 and garnered raves in the *New York Times, Wall Street Journal* and many international

---

[34] alloneera.com/liluinterview

publications.[35] These extremely encouraging beginnings fortified the vision I had in the pool in Bedford and in the temples of Thailand, and even fortified my career switch from eco-developer to grape grower. I told a Greek restaurant owner in Chicago, who sipped Cipes Brut, that my name, Cipes, had been shortened from Tsipes to Cipes when my ancestors came over from Greece. He exclaimed, "Oh, Tsipes, that's the leftover grapes that you make Tsipouro with, which is like Grappa from Italy!" I was being Guided on many levels! My name meant leftover grapes! The Summerhill winery expanded and began winning the top awards all over the world. The conclusive experiments studying the effect of sacred geometry on liquids would soon require a larger pyramid as our growing loyal fans were demanding that all our wines, not just the sparkling wines, be pyramid energized.

My mission was clear, I was to devote myself to studying the properties of the most precise, largest, man-made structure on the planet: **The Great Pyramid**, a.k.a. **The Cheops Pyramid**, Cairo, Egypt. I began experimenting with wooden, open-frame pyramids, oriented to exact true North, and with the same angles as The Great Pyramid and with the precision angles of the hips and fusion to the base and apex. We proved that orange juice, water and wine were all clarified and either had their flavor enhanced or had their imperfections brought out. We also showed that unhomogenized milk would turn to yogurt, while a glass of the same milk, not in an open-frame pyramid, turned rancid. Time lapse photography was used to prove that plants grew in a clockwise motion versus helter-skelter a few feet away without the pyramid. In those experiments, we made the startling discovery that not only the properties of the products were clarified, but that the apparent effect was accomplished in an open-frame pyramid with no sides, showing that it was the frame that was effective. After proving that the open-frame wooden pyramid models we had built to test the effects of sacred geometry on liquids and on plant growth patterns had all been conclusive, I was Guided to visit The Great Pyramid again.

On my third trip to Cairo to study The Great Pyramid, I asked my famous guide, John Anthony West, the self-described "Rogue" Egyptologist who starred with Charlton Heston in the Emmy-

---

[35] alloneera.com/raves

Award winning NBC Special, *Mystery of the Sphinx*, to accompany me. I asked him to give me his scholarly research on how The Great Pyramid was built. This was music to his ears. He opened up to me with the excitement of his discoveries of the water marks around The Sphinx, showing geologically that The Sphinx and The Great Pyramid would have had to have been built many thousands of years before the history book's dates of The Cheops (Khufu) era of the kings (26th Century BC). John Anthony would not speculate a specific date, but we mused that it could easily be 20,000-50,000 years ago when the Nile was in a closer location. We also mused that an ancient civilization, who had technology we don't have today, must have built The Great Pyramid. Today's technology would not allow us to even move stones that huge, much less fuse them to each other in absolute precision, with no mortar. It was then that the clear message was gifted to me (just like in the vision in Thailand) that we could build a fused-frame pyramid to the same proportions as the open, wooden frame pyramids that showed us such phenomenal results. Upon my return from Cairo, I designed an open-frame, four-story, sixty-foot-square, continuous-pour pyramid, using high density concrete (50 mpg versus the normal 35 mpg) and fiberglass rebar from underwater construction so that we wouldn't introduce ferrous metals (steel) into the concrete, which would re-orient the alignment to magnetic North versus true North. The final pour of concrete fused the frame together and created the full energetic effect of the pyramid. That day we all felt the jolt of the final pour, creating the fused frame, precision pyramid, when all seven of our watches stopped, I immediately got down on my knees, and kissed the earth as a gesture of gratuity for my Divine Guidance and all of my blessings.

Today, more than twenty years later, John Anthony West's discoveries about the age of the Sphinx and The Great Pyramid are being verified by geologists, engineers and other experts in relevant fields. In fact, very recent studies present a near-indisputable case for the Nile having completely changed course, as John Anthony had suggested[36]. These studies have also revealed massive water weathering marks around the Sphinx. Since scientific studies show there has been no water to speak of on the Plateau since perhaps as many as thirty-thousand years ago, and certainly a minimum of ten-thousand years, the true age of the Sphinx and the Great and other Giza Pyramids

---

[36] See alloneera.com/pyramidcode

may certainly be many thousands of years older than the present history books tell us.

There is also a very famous reading from The Sleeping Prophet, Edgar Cayce (A.R.E. Association of Research and Enlightenment in Virginia Beach, VA) where he places The Hall of Records of The Atlantean Civilization under the right paw of The Sphinx. Today, seismic soundings reveal that there is a vault under The Sphinx' paws but despite urging, the antiquities department in Cairo has refused permission to excavate[37].

The Great Pyramid and the Summerhill Pyramid are both built to 51.8⁻4° angles and are Pi and Phi. In relation to a circle, they have the properties of a precision sacred geometry chamber. One could deduce that they and others built these exact proportions, which are our hearts and souls represented in a structure. Our very DNA strands and all the atoms that make up our cells are related to the pyramid shape. The four sides are the four directions as well as the four elements: earth, air, fire, and water. Each of the four sides has three points, for a total that equates to the twelve houses of the zodiac. Chapter 34, "The Four Faces of God," in *Initiation* by Elisabeth Haich, reveals the significance of these sacred chambers brilliantly[38]! Often called ascension chambers, a precision replica of the Great Pyramid, built without ferrous metals and oriented to true north, are now proven to have an intense clarifying effect on all liquids. We humans are mostly liquid! In Summerhill's twenty-five-year experiment on the effect of sacred geometry on liquids we have made a breakthrough discovery. Water, juice, milk, wine, and we humans become clarified. The essence of the liquid, the characteristics of it, become more pronounced. This opens up a very interesting aside. Could it be that the pyramid chamber amplifies our personal individual characteristics, our soul purpose and mission? In vino veritas (in wine there is truth) – in pyramids there is truth.

We cellar all Summerhill wines in the pyramid chamber and have proven conclusively that they become clarified. If we put a wine with flaws in the pyramid, the flaws become accentuated. We have learned to lab test all our wines for flaws before cellaring in the chamber through the VQA

---

[37] See alloneera.com/edgarcayce
[38] Please go to alloneera.com/initiation to see a scan of the chapter.

(Vintners Quality Alliance) certification. A wine with pure nature characteristics becomes enhanced. We have hosted blind side-by-side tastings of the same wine, served at the same temperature, for over twenty-five years, and each and every time have the astonishing results: everyone acknowledges that they are different and more than ninety percent select and declare the pyramid cellared wine as being softer, cleaner, more aromatic and more flavorful! The most memorable taste test was broadcasted live internationally on CBC Radio, when a pitcher of frozen organic orange juice had been made the night before and two glasses were poured from the pitcher. One was placed in the pyramid chamber and one was placed in the office of the winery. During the live broadcast, ten people blind tasted from the two glasses and each one chose the pyramid juice as tasting and smelling more like fresh squeezed juice. Summerhill.bc.ca contains a section about the pyramid with many fascinating details. The experiment continues actively with scientific lab equipment being introduced to test the wines so that sensory evaluation is not the only criteria for judging the remarkable phenomena.

At Summerhill, we have developed what we call "A Pyramid Experience Tour" where, at the option of the tour guide, the group is invited to turn off their cellphones and take deep breaths before entering the chamber. They are reminded that we are electrical in nature and that as we relax our thinking by focusing on the breath and "letting go," we have an opportunity to expand our "Field" and come into our hearts. We suggest they enter quietly and take a seat with their feet on the floor and their eyes closed and just sit for a few minutes in total stillness and silence with the tour guide gently breaking the silence. For most, entering a space of sacred geometry induces an instant meditation and an invitation to be in total peace. Many have exclaimed that they felt as if they were stepping into a different world. The most voiced comments are that they felt removed from all distractions and influences – a total "get-away." It is often compared to a return to the womb, a homecoming, and a place where we want to be and don't want to leave! This is when the guides have to joke with them and coax them to come for "the best part of the tour": the actual tasting of the pyramid-energized wines!

The Summerhill Pyramid is second only to The Great Pyramid of Egypt for precision and alignment. Its sacred geometry chamber is perhaps the most conducive chamber in North America in which to go within. The definition of 'going within' is written on the parchment scroll from Baird T. Spalding's (1872-1953) *Life of the Masters of the Far East*, displayed in the entrance vestibule of the pyramid:

To guard against destruction or subversion, people built twelve corresponding Bibles in stone and located them through the Motherland. In order to bring them together under one head, thus making the precepts everlasting, they built The Great Pyramid thus proving that the Christ, the foundation of civilization, was solidly established on earth among men and could not be defaced or erased. It would last forever, not only as a beacon that would hold high the light, but as a reflector for that light. It not only reflected the light but gave forth the oft repeated command, 'if Humanity has lost the light, go within; there you will find recorded the precepts that will renew the light so that it may shine forth from you, the lost sheep that are wandering bereft of light'

Excerpt from LIFE & TEACHING of the Masters of the Far East, Volume 3 by Baird T. Spalding, 1872-1953

As soon as the pyramid was completed in December 1997, we began hosting gatherings, starting with the Spring Equinox on March 21, 1998, and we have hosted a "packed house" for each Solstice and Equinox since. From the pivotal Winter Solstice on December 21, 2012 onward, we have also initiated full and new moon gatherings. Groups of well over a hundred women are gathering to celebrate each new moon, while the men gather around the sacred fire[39] in the Summerhill Makwala Memorial Kekuli; and well over one hundred and fifty men, women, and children are gathering for full moon celebrations! They are joining together to meditate, chant, drum, dance, feast, and further open their Receiving Selves in each other's bands of energy. More and more amazing images have begun to emerge: pictures depicting beaming circles, balls of light, orbs and projections of rays of bright energy from the corners of the pyramid.[40]

Many photos of dancing green beams and copious bright energetic hues of color merging as one in bright white were captured. It seems as though there is a communication-taking place that transcends the five senses. The alloneera.com website features many of these astonishing images and there is a photograph of a captured light phenomenon coming from the apex of the pyramid, which is now the cover of this book. It was taken by a Chartered Management Accountant (CMA) who signed a document verifying the photo is untouched. While there are technical explanations for orbs, especially from cameras with LED flash, the enormity of the phenomena warrants mention. The images also remind us that there are illusions of what time is. Time is affected by the fact that we are spinning at over 25,000 miles an hour orbiting our star. Also, there is a remarkable increase in orbs when the subjects are in "spiritual practices".

In the Now, we merge and communicate with all there is, both on our human material plane and in the spiritual realms of which we are eternally a part. In the Now, we see our magnificent plane of demonstration, our emerald planet, and behold the moment-to-moment genius that we collectively manifest. We are cognizant that each and every one of the almost eight billion of us are "planetary citizens" with an all-one holistic consciousness. We are one world of beings, individually and collectively projecting unmistakable rays of light with magnitude and potential far grander than seeing ourselves as separate, as individuals, countries, ethnic groups, or even as a distinct planet. There is no separation. We realize that we are ALL ONE!

---

[39] See allonera.com/sacredfire

[40] See alloneera.com/orbs

As Dr. Valerie Hunt has so brilliantly documented, our bands of energy expanding, not only in sacred geometry chambers or around sacred fires, but also whenever we join together with a lofty purpose, sharing pure intentions. We feel our energy expand in. They are uniquely relaxing our ego selves and welcoming the Loving Universal Consciousness (LUC), which is most at home and flourishing in these chambers. These gatherings, when observed globally, are perhaps THE stepping-stone we desperately need to return to our Selves!

While creating internal and external portals for the purity of love to flow through our individual Selves, we are coming together in collective receivership, welcoming colossal rejuvenating energies. The momentum has begun to catapult this glorious era with the establishment of branches of the Summerhill Model all over the globe. We can now vastly expand these amplifications of healing **worldwide!**

Perhaps the establishment of gatherings in highly conducive, sacred geometry chambers serves to open the ideal and much needed path to rejuvenating our souls and our planet on a grand scale.

One of the many extraordinary happenings in the pyramid occurred in 2001, when I invited the Rosicrucian Grand Masters from around the world to enjoy Summerhill as the venue for their annual Grand Masters Gathering. While I was not yet a fellow Master, or even formally a Rosicrucian, they honored me with an invitation to join them. There, the Senior Grand Master led us through a guided meditation. Step-by-step, she led us through our bodies, from our toes to our feet; from our feet to our knees; up through our legs to our core centers; upward through to our hearts, neck, jaw, eyes, crown chakra; and then to the apex of the pyramid. At the very moment when she brought us from our crown chakras to the apex of the pyramid, there was a giant crack of thunder! The skies opened up immediately and heavy rain began pouring through the vent holes around the pyramid apex! The angle of the rain must have been perpendicular to the apex to allow it to come gushing through the vents, which had never happened before! This astounding cleansing phenomenon will be remembered and shall be on the lips of thousands of Rosicrucians all over the world, for all time.

Another fascinating phenomenon occurred when I was entertaining a team of scientists from London, England for dinner. That evening, there were fifteen newspaper, television and radio reporters in the dining room, as well as a pianist. In between courses, I suggested to my four guests and the wife of the pianist that we have a quick visit to the pyramid. We lit a candle on the barrel that was in the center of the pyramid and the six of us made a circle and put our hands up to each other without touching. Suddenly, the flame of the candle began to leap into the air. At this moment one of the scientists let out a huge yelp and put his hands down. He showed us a pyramid-shaped burn on his right hand, just below his index finger and exclaimed that he would like to leave the pyramid as soon as possible. Upon returning to the dining room, we shared the experience with the media people at the table next to us and they all took pictures of the burn and made notes of the incident. For months, I begged the scientist to share with me what was going on in his head when he got the burn, but he refused to tell me. Finally, one day I picked up the phone and called him in London and said, "Anthony, I really need to know what was going through you when you got that burn." After a long pause, he revealed that he had been teleporting. In other words, at that exact moment, he was standing in both the Summerhill Pyramid and in the Taj Mahal at the same time. Today, more than ten years later, he still has the scar of the pyramid on his hand.

There are countless colossal phenomena always happening in the pyramid including the miraculous healing of a brain tumor! A Summerhill tour guides' father, who was a prominent public servant, was stricken with a terminal brain tumor and was given just a few months to live. Our tour guide suggested that he come to the pyramid. After much coaxing, his father arrived and was introduced to the ideas of vibrational healing and to the concept that we are our own best healers. It was then that he contacted a cellist in Europe who was famous for shrinking tumors with his instrument and he sponsored him to come to Kelowna, British Columbia, to be with him in the pyramid. After three days of sessions in the pyramid, his tumor miraculously began to shrink and he was able to resume his very high-profile job for many years.

A great breakthrough also happened at Summerhill at the Spring Equinox Gathering on March 20, 2015, when we built a portable pyramid made with light beams, which were rented for $200. We built a fire in the middle, and the beams highlighted the smoke and created a beautiful and precisely-

146

angled pyramid, which could be expanded to almost any size. The technology to create low-cost portable light pyramids, is answered prayer in the quest to develop economically feasible sacred geometry chambers for gatherings all over the world!

Portable pyramid made with light beams.

Introducing sacred geometry to classrooms, nursing homes, jails, hospital rooms, housing, offices, food and beverage producers, and most of all, meditation spaces, is a noble passion, now achievable. Imagine the effect of a sacred geometry influence, which strengthens our creativeness. We could nourish our electrical-in-nature bodies with negative ionized "charging spaces with positive ions that put us to sleep! There is a wonderful story about a young family who built a precision pyramid house and invited their elderly parents to come and live with them. A remarkable thing happened to the father. Obviously his hormones were stimulated and his white hair began to have color and he felt a youthful vigor and decided to go out to work! They also noted that their food stayed fresher without refrigeration and that they all enjoyed less sickness and vigorous health.

There is a Grand Thesis emerging, where consciousness reigns. Gatherings are a model that can be established in communities all around the world, in any and all languages. For perhaps the first time in recorded history, we are co-creating a viable platform that is conducive to our coming together as Ascending Beings, to heal our Earth through the expansion of consciousness. By uniting as like-minded, like-hearted souls we create a crescendo of Grand Purpose, where we can purify and manifest on all scales and all levels. While most of the Summerhill gatherings have been planned by a committee while we welcomed guest speakers / facilitators, some of the most powerful events have been those Guided spontaneously.

On a crisp January night, the full moon peering through a few scattered evening clouds, I stood in front of ninety souls gathered in the pyramid. Where there had previously been elaborate formalities in preparation, that night only a single carpet was laid on the floor in the pyramid, centering us in the heart directions of north, south, east, and west, up to "Father Sky" and down to "Mother Earth," with only six candles. I played the native drum, and my guest, Teresa Rambold, accompanied me with a custom-made, oversized, keyless Autoharp that she played like a dulcimer[41]. Then, spontaneously, a suggestion was introduced by Rome Donati that each one of the ninety of us share what it was they truly loved. This opened a lively stream of discussion. Some spoke of loving others, their pets, life, themselves, and each of the heartfelt expressions were followed by an enthusiastic *a-ho!* – an

---

[41] Theresa Rambold: alloneera.com/taoe

Okanagan language affirmation. The magnificence of this sharing progression was the continuous repetition and clarification of the word *love*, and with that, the phenomena of a natural bursting of ecstatic enthusiasm that was so totally felt among us! The entire group felt the jolt. We acknowledged that our words were only as profound as our own experiences, as we collectively beheld the vibration created that night. That spontaneous night, we pooled our genius potentials and took back our power to be the Gods and Goddesses we are. We shared in a grand ascension!

This experience reminds me that we have an expansion of ascension every time we experience a jolt. To give you an example, I have a practice of often going into my beloved vineyard and holding one plant with both of my hands. I become one with that vine, merging its essence with my essence. I actually say to the plant the words emphatically out loud: *From the Lord God of my being, unto the Lord God of your being; indeed, I salute the divinity within you! Namaste! May you flourish and produce to the grandest of your essence and purpose, in the greatest peace and comfort of your being! Indeed!* I then pause, allowing the vine and me to meld together as one. I then forcefully voice, *SO BE IT, AND SO IT IS!* The closure is immediately established in the jolt that is felt and reverberated between the two of us. I then take this wondrous, captured, powerful energy with the vine, and pronounce that this love between us, be bestowed on *all* plants, on *all* trees, and indeed throughout *all* of nature, *all* over the planet! A permanent union, a foundation of profound significance, is established! It is revealed that our declaration of love to all plants could not have such powerful impact without the initial jolt of the merger of the two of us established first. This magnificent demonstration of our all-powerful, unlimited love is easily demonstrated in so many varieties of situations. Knowing how powerful experiencing profound love for one child is, one can then project this same, pure one-to-one blessing on all the children of the world. This really applies to anyone or any living thing that you give your heart to. This can be extended to all living entities. As an example, I had this meditation on the anniversary of my dear departed sister on her birthday:

Today's early morning meditation
Brought me deeper understanding
Of the meaning of having a sister
As I refreshed my memories
Of our closeness
And of our differences
I felt so blessed
I became one with my sister

I then felt that oneness
With all sisters
Billions of them
I blessed them all
In a chant that came through me
With grandness that touched me
And the world

We are beginning to merge both the grassroots and all the diplomatic options and progress rapidly toward returning our planet to its natural state. Gatherings at the occurrence of new moons, full moons, the two Equinoxes, and Solstices, and creating a central council and a series of local councils, is creating our grassroots foundation and catapulting us back to a state of grand healing, receivership, and pure love. Stepping forth, we are choosing to purify, open, and honor our very essence. We are grand entities in a grand universe and our all-powerful purpose becomes alive, a might clearing and blessing!

A huge momentum is touching each and every heart with loving reverence for our living planet. We are reuniting in our eternal soul memory, echoing our intentions and our revelations through receiving and giving back to the ever present Loving Universal Consciousness...that we are!

As we gather and dance in celebration, we are moved to the point of leaping to rejoice in our continuous advancements in consciousness. We have within, everything we need to heal our Selves and our planet; and, as we each join the joyous momentum, we discover a deepening pride in our new awareness, our fervent quest for peace, and our powerful collective nurturing and ever-increasing harmony with our beloved Mother Earth and all of Her majestic creatures. Selah!

Stephen and Caroline Myss after exchanging "I love you's."

152

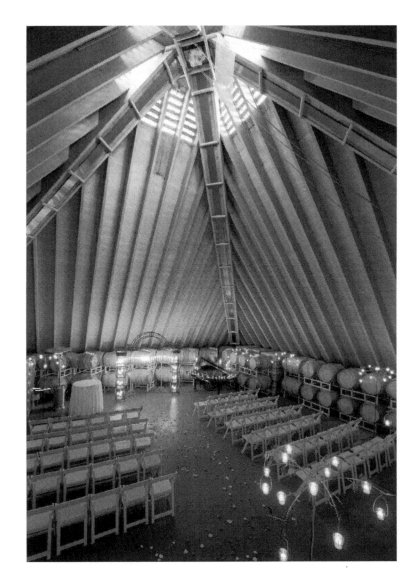

Inside the Summerhill Pyramid.
Py-ra-mid: fire in the middle
Photo Credit: Kevin Trowbridge

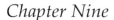

Chapter Nine

HEART-CENTERED LEADERSHIP

Leadership, leadership, what is involved in leadership? How do we get the most impact to the most people in the most efficient way? Do teens that set themselves on fire to let the world know their dire dismay at the invasion of their leadership in Tibet have an impact? Do the multitude of books, plays, art, music, articles, and examples by so many millions of genius-inspired souls or Light Workers have an impact? The sad fact is, in spite of today's grandest communication technology and our being able to share our genius level Knowingness, we are simultaneously at the peak of our darkest hour. Corporate greed and preoccupation with "the human drama" are both at an all-time high.

Who shall lead us now? Who shall lead us when it is all too late? Who shall lead us when chaos pervades? Who shall lead us when the entire population is clouded by delusion, engrossed so completely in the human drama, overwhelmed, and tuned out of all but the constant cravings for food, physical comforts, and material pleasures? And when we can't satiate these cravings? As my dad would say, "When people are hungry, they go to war." What will a war do? Considering today's atomic war technology, it may lead to the horrific potential for the demise of all life. We are still strongly influenced by the past era that, was at its height created the first and only new paradigm: we humans now have the ability to annihilate ourselves, completely by triggering a Nuclear Winter. We are at the tipping point; our hearts, minds, and souls are uniting to reset our present treacherous path. The Earth is cleansing herself as we ascend in our oneness with her and all there is. Our re-connection is all powerful! When just one of us has a "jolt" of realization, it is felt by all there is!

In 1962, at the age of eighteen, I earned my Real Estate Broker's license and launched myself as an entrepreneur. In the business of land development, I felt at one with the Earth, my Earth. I'd see logging trucks driving down the highway full of trees and I'd cringe. I had resounding remembrance of the days when people and trees were friends. To this day, I still cry out for my trees every time I see logging trucks. Being in the business of buying, developing and reselling land gave me a position of partnership with the land…I could protect the Earth! It allowed me a portal through which to become an innovator for a balance between development and ecological sustainability. I became a pioneer in saving steep slopes and wetlands, at a time when there were no ordinances that said a developer must do so. It all stemmed from a deep love for the land. I wanted my children to grow up in a world where people allowed the food chain to naturally continue and the land and trees around the houses to support nature, and I promoted my vision to local municipalities, with seminars led by engineers that I hired. I introduced a concept of cluster zoning allowing wetlands to be left unaltered as a vital part of the food chain, and protecting steep slopes, allowing them to keep forests and animals undisturbed. I knew if there were a way to save our planet from mindless destruction, it was (and is) through our individual and collective heart-centered leadership.

Fast forward to the early 1990s, during the very heated stages of the environmental movement. At that time, I welcomed the world's leading seed producers into my home on the Summerhill eighty-acre organic vineyard. Twenty-six of us gathered for a four-day immersion. We had presentations from well-known seed company presidents and from two First Nations Elders. We learned the shocking facts about how grave our environmental situation was becoming. We joined together and witnessed heart-wrenching video accounts of scores of East Indian farmers who could no longer support their families and were committing suicide, as huge companies like Monsanto with their genetically modified organism (GMO) products ended generations of organic farming businesses.

Every one of the seed producers and Elders enthusiastically shared the boundless potentials of humanity and all life thriving with pure organic growing practices versus chemical and GMO farming. We all clearly saw our very "capacity to function" as human beings diminished by the malnutrition and dehydration caused by GMO foods, along with the devastation of toxins threatening all of life. We all knew that wholesome organic food and pure water are essential for us to live in Divine Guidance. It is a safe assumption to say that in the short span of the last thirty odd years since the original seed producers gathered in my home, our "divine connection", shrunk at an alarming rate. This reality is due not only to the destruction and depletion of love in the food we eat, air we breathe, and water we drink, but simultaneously to the paralleled increase of entrapment in fear-based human drama – the veil that separates us from our divine heritage.

Those in attendance for the presentations held the original seeds of the Earth, from all around the world. They were the guardians of the seeds that are naturally evolved and unaltered by technology. As a group, we proactively brought forth our united intentions to raise the Earth's vibration, to maintain the essence of the seeds, knowing that doing so would allow our crops to continue to flourish and grow to touch the lives of billions. Discussions flowed, weaving in the enthusiastically shared knowledge that pure organic nutrition was the fundamental basis for rich healthy bodies as vessels and conduits of Spirit-centered peace, joy, love, and abundance, and that this vision for the planet and ourselves stood at high risk, as it is now at the hands of profit-driven corporations. Fueled by the impact of the devastation of the natural world, and by nature's and our ability to rejuvenate, my frustration mounted and I saw a vision clearly appear before me in answer. While the heavy hearts of the seed producers were calling for a massive global consciousness raising, I beheld an epiphany that will stay with me forever. I actually *saw* the silver cord, that connects us all. It was shrinking rapidly at the hand of the toxicity, pollution, and lack of vibrant nutrients that was upon us all. I watched our silver cords with pure Spirit being shrunken and compromised because we were no longer able to vibrate in our natural harmonic state with nature. I witnessed this cord, described as the Kundalini energy in Eastern traditions, and by individuals who have had near-death experiences. In my vision, the cord was a pulsing vibration in snake-like formation. I heard and saw Light and tone ring lively through it. It connects our spinal column to our medulla oblongata and continues through our crown chakra, the top of our skulls.

In this pivotal "time in our times", we are passionate about bringing this vital awareness to all, so we can see and feel how urgent it is that we restore and fortify our connective channels in all possible ways. The most important factor is to maintain our bodies' vibrational essence in order to receive and be connected to Spirit. We must return to having our food be organic, ingesting no GMO or processed foods, and drinking pure water. The vast treachery of chemical corporate farming that has come into being toward the end of this last material-centered era, is that it has been saturated into almost every product commercially produced today. **Without eating organic whole foods, we are rapidly losing the ability of our souls in these bodies to fully resonate with the Loving Universal Consciousness. This unprecedented departure is the crux of our present dilemma. We are in dire need of restoring our bodies and souls back into full vibratory potential.**

I am still undaunted in my plea for everyone to grasp the essence of organics in spite of so little progress after over thirty years of Summerhill's leadership, winning gold medals and trophies around the world and bringing pride and fame to British Columbia. There are only less than 3% of the over 300 wineries certified organic in British Columbia. This is a far North cool climate region that flourishes with organic practices! We have been publicly expounding the urgencies for maintaining wholesomeness for the Earth, the children, the elderly, and the health of our pristine eighty-mile-long Okanagan Lake, which is one of the most significant supplies of drinking water to the valley and has one of the slowest turnover systems. Sadly, economics, the almighty dollar, has taken precedence with almost all of the wineries vying to optimize production with chemicals, when in fact, organic practices improve production through being naturally healthy and resistant to disease! Wines produced from chemically grown grapes have been tested to all have toxins and that is a travesty. We now have proof that a moderate amount of organic wine is a health elixir, especially enjoyed with a meal, supplying an abundance of live nutrients. Organically grown wines also have the highest amounts of antioxidants and deserve a place alongside pure water and organic fruit juices. As importantly, the chemicals used in grape growing are extremely toxic to the water, the air, the Earth, and us! We are now leading a conversion of all of the vineyards and orchards, and all of the residences, school yards and municipal bi-ways in the Okanagan Valley, to be organic. The fact that our tiny fruit growing region is so far north gives us the advantage of having the least pests, therefore making it the easiest to manage organically. Imagine having the northernmost fruit growing region in the world, where the content of the anti-oxidant nutrients in the fruits and vegetables is the highest possible, be a model for the world as a diamond on our emerald planet!

CEO Ezra Cipes, Co-founder and Winemaker Eric von Krosigk, and Proprietor Stephen Cipes

Summerhill Pyramid Winery wins Canadian Wine Producer of the Year at The International Wine Competition in London, England in December 2009 and a separate award for Double Gold Best Sparkling Wine.

Recent wins include an unprecedented 100-point double gold at the San Francisco International Wine Competition with 32 countries participating. June 2017 and BEST CHARDONNAY IN THE WORLD at the Chardonnay du Monde in Burgundy, France with over 700 entries from 38 countries.

Sadly, less than 3% of the 300 wineries are organic in spite of our proof that organic wine tastes better and IS way better for our bodies and for the planet.

The 2020 Vision to convert all of the pristine wilderness valley to organic has arrived as a world model of harmony with nature by aiming to have the entire residential, agricultural and municipal lands be 100% organic by the year 2020. The DECLARATION has now been signed by thousands and can be signed online at organicokanagan.com. As of this writing, it has been signed by most of the mayors and First Nations chiefs, the majority of the Water Forum Board, and thousands of others, including celebrities Marianne Williamson, David Suzuki and Robert Bateman (who also publicly declared their support). Please sign online today. Visit organicokanagan.com for more information, including a video showing a comparison of chemical to organic wine on CHBCTV. Initiated with great enthusiasm at the 10th annual Okanagan Organic Festival on September 27, 2015, the Declaration is gaining momentum daily!

Organic departments in supermarkets across North America and Europe have more than doubled in size and popularity. The recent takeover of Whole Foods Organic Markets by Amazon may help to catapult our consumption of whole foods by lowering prices with increased volume of sales. The market for organic wine is the fastest growing segment of the wine industry worldwide. The quest has been launched! This is the ideal time to urgently demonstrate that economic and ecological abundance thrive together using organic farming methods. We want to return to growing our own gardens, we want to be self-sufficient, we want to get away from dependence and from giving away our power!

It is our clarity and shared vision that awakens us to not waste paper that is made from the trees that give us our biosphere, to not buy glossy magazines and paper that has been bleached with chemicals that are killing our fish, and to incorporate reusable products instead of continuing to throw away countless coffee cups, plastic bottles and metal containers that lead to animals' suffering and mountains of garbage. We are the only species on the planet creating garbage. We seem to be crazed with insisting on elaborate packaging for everything we produce. The "shift" is upon us! We are no longer willing to tolerate abuse of our precious resources. We are modifying them to minimums, as we merge and ascend into Divine Guidance. We are returning home to our deserved place of joy and abundance, a celebration of forever loving consciousness!

As we merge, we naturally start to be self-sufficient; want to grow our own food, and no longer support packaged products or needless planetary destruction of any kind. Esther Sands and Sean Sands, MD, have built a model of what they term a "closed-loop." The Sean and Esther Sanctuary is a twenty-five-acre model of self-sufficiency, an economically independent community, nestled in the wilderness area of Grand Forks, British Columbia. Everything, including all human waste, goes back into the soil and creates compost for future life. They are bringing to our attention that we have created an extraordinary burden on the planet with the impact of the way we treat our human excretion. It is but one of the aspects they have demonstrated in their world model. They have also demonstrated how to live without hardly any money, including an ingenious way to build year-round residences for little more than the cost of the nails[42].

We all have a calling to allow ourselves to be the conduits we naturally are, no matter what influences and illusions we come from.

~

The movements and intentions we initiate ripple through all of eternity consciously and perpetually. Welcoming the All One Era moves into fifth-dimensional consciousness. **For the first time (and possibly the last time), we have the means of saving our planet, because when we are in full receivership, bathing in Knowingness, we Know how to nurture and demonstrate our harmony with The Mother.** We are now co-creating an accord for humanity to step back and to take back our unified power and glory. More than a grassroots movement, this essential return to our Ascended Selves is our precious opportunity to preserve life as we know it. Every human resonates with his or her soul memory; every soul knows that we are all one with the Holy Presence and every religion and ascended Master has cited this clearly. More importantly, stepping into our leadership with unified intentions of pure love, is what we give to ourselves.

---

[42] See *Greening the Cube* at alloneera.com/greeningthecube, which shows how to build a year-round house for under two-hundred dollars!

Don't give up on finding the leader – you have found him/her. It is you.

~

Returning our Bodies to the Rhythms of Nature

We are now naturally redeveloping the instincts that lead us back to being in harmony with nature. They are not laws or restrictions, but rather powerful intentions from those who are practicing them and realizing the greatest of awakenings and openings. Our powerful individual leadership is SO needed now versus giving our power to government.

Today, almost all of the Earth's natural resources are controlled by governments and corporations who are guided by supply and demand, however we are not all on "the same page". In 2016, the Canadian government approved a major curtailing of coal production by the year 2030, while the U.S. has put coal miners back to work at the time of this writing. The news that a 7.4 magnitude earthquake hit Fukushima, Japan on November 21, 2016 aggravating the already out of control previous catastrophe of a nine magnitude quake hitting the nuclear power plant there on March 11, 2011. There continues to be a huge spewing of radiation to all of the food chain through acid rain, causing global effects to the fish and ocean life. Such a rate of exploitation is far in excess of what our Earth can sustain. While there are many who endeavor to develop land in full recognition of nature's harmony, there also remains greed as never before, with huge mining, clear cut logging, striping of steep slopes, building of pipelines, and pollution of wetlands and lakes contributing daily to the loss of animal and plant species, and threatening Indigenous people's habitat and the continued existence of all of civilization. Heart-centered leadership is the beacon of Light most needed now.

The **All One Era** has an opportunity to create an official AOE stamp of approval on products and services to all be in harmony with the Earth and with our collective intention of eternal abundance.

By creating a roster of All One Era Certified Goods and Services traded online, a huge reduction in costs will evolve and an awakening to products and services that are taking from our earth will be revealed. In fact, a worldwide ALL ONE ERA online marketing network has the potential to eliminate big box stores and other online sales with their retail mark-ups, and provide a vital "evening out" of prices for all consumers. A system of contra versus monetary exchange for goods and services is also a major goal. Establishing gathering venues worldwide is the major priority. Contact alloneera.com/council or stephen@alloneera.com or call 1-833-ALL-1-ERA to launch a gathering venue in your community.

The All One Era Sacred Fire

In ceremony around the sacred fire, where the Presence of "all my relations" is honored and celebrated, the First Nations people call upon the grandmothers and grandfathers for Guidance. The Indigenous peoples have lived in harmony with the land for eons and are the natural stewards of the Earth. A treasured example is the legacy of the mighty Blackfoot Nation, whose vast territory stretched from the entirety of the province of Alberta, and included many parts of British Columbia and Montana in the United States. They had a sacred tradition of constantly being on the move, so that they would never scar the Earth with their settlements. They, and all the Aboriginal peoples (which, if we go back far enough, is ALL of us!), were and are to this day, a people deeply connected with the cosmos. Our deep-rooted tribal love for the Earth is awakened. If not now, when shall we burst out with our all-powerful love?

The sacred fire can be built in the center of a portable light beam pyramid! It can be established in a pit house or Kekuli. The reverence for the Presence of the Grandmothers and Grandfathers on the other side to "come through" is all that is required.

~

When Alex Janvier (82), the famous indigenous artist, one of the famous Eight Indigenous Artists in Canada, came to visit the Makwala Memorial Kekuli at Summerhill, for an invitation to have an evening of drumming and storytelling around the sacred fire in July of 2017, he and his wife Jacqueline and I were the only ones who showed up. This gave us the opportunity to get to know each other over dinner and after hearing that he was the son of the last tribal chief of the Dene Nation, the largest square mile tribal nation in North America, which ran from the Eskimo region in the far North, all the way to South America, he went on to reiterate that the Canadian government's genocide program called the Residential Schools, tore him and his siblings away from their father and usurped him, making him the last of the series of chiefs over perhaps thousands of years. It was then that I decided to gift him a copy of this manuscript and invited him to join us at a new moon gathering the following week. He began reading the book immediately and joined me in the Kekuli on the new moon. He sat silently as fourteen men (it's men only in the Kekuli and women only in the pyramid on the new moon) picked up the talking stick and spoke to the fire as we do. Then he leaned over to me and asked if he could go up and take the stick and talk to the fire. I said, "Yes, of course!" Well, he exclaimed that for the first time in many years his hearing came back to him and that when I spoke he heard every word clearly and his deafness was healed! Three days later I received a phone call from him that he and his wife just returned to their home in Cold Lake, Alberta, and that he had finished reading the manuscript on the plane and that his hearing was still fully healed and most importantly, he thanked me for reminding him of so many of the wisdoms that his father had taught to him and all of the people in their tribe before the Residential Schools uprooted everything. I promised to visit him and see his brilliant art studio and flew up to Edmonton and drove the four hours North to be with him and his wife, Jacqueline. I was inspired to do a documentary on his career as an artist and on his excitement to pick up where his father left off where the people honored the earth with such devotion and reverence that they moved their territories rather than scar her with permanent structures, much like the Blackfoot Nation, which was also a huge territory. Even though there is no longer a hereditary chief of the Dene Nation, I call him Chief Alex and I encourage everyone to see his wonderful face and his years of inspirational artwork at alexjanvier.com.

As Heart-Centered Leaders...

We have an opportunity to draft an accord between nations that will preserve our precious resources and ensure they are perpetuated for future generations. Such an accord is drafted below as an example and an inspiration for us to actually move swiftly to incorporate such lofty, loving accords throughout the world.

Establishing an International Accord between nations purchasing resources such as China, and nations such as Canada and its respective First Nations within, who are rich in resources, opens the opportunity for a new paradigm of sustainability.

DRAFT
INTERNATIONAL ACCORD

Declaration

The Undersigned:
Environmental Activist, Dr. David Suzuki, Representing Planet Earth,

Son of Village Tribal Chief Chanunt of the Osoyoos Nation, Moose AKA Ron Hall
Representing Canada and all First Nations,

Grand Master and Hollywood Actor, Stephen Cheng, Representing China, and;

Stephen Cipes, Representing The All One Era.

We speak for Planet Earth, whom we all have had a part in co-creating.
We hereby recognize the essence and precious opportunity our Planet Paradise represents by
allowing our physical bodies to materialize and express and collectively enrich our forever souls.

We hereby recognize that sadly, we now face a time when our Earth is severely threatened, even to the point of total loss of life at our hands.

All humans, plants, animals, rivers, and oceans now suffer extraordinary conditions and are in extreme states of stress. The demands for her natural resources have peaked, and the use of them has created mass pollution that has choked the survival of countless species and surpassed her ability to rejuvenate and heal without immediate relief of the demands on her.

The Elders of the Inca Nation have had their minyan and have cited:
- The disappearance of the condor during the 1980s.
- The disappearance of the mountaintop lagoons in the mid-1990s.
- The wrath of the sun with the disappearance of the ozone layer in the 1990s.
The Hopi Elders have prophesied that the ancient line on the rock wall separates on December 2012 into two choices for humankind: One line continues up, which represents the continuation of our present aggressive material consumption, and the other line returns down to our original consciousness of harmony, peace, joy and abundance.

All of the plants, animals, humans, and our Mother Earth Herself are joining together into a concert of highest vibration as we lift the veil in this new era of welcoming our oneness and opening to receiving the Loving Universal Consciousness we all bathe in.
In this sacred hour of Presence, Patience and Fortitude, we hereby set forth:

This <u>DECLARATION</u> on behalf of Planet Earth, as an entity.

We hereby decree to henceforth and forever more, adopt "planet-centric criteria" to the consumption of all-natural resources vs. "human-centric." This encompasses, but is not limited to all foods, oil, gas, coal, metals, timber, and water harvested from Earth.

We, as citizens of the Earth and as established Nations who trade money and services for natural resources, hereby agree to abide by this Accord from this day forward, as a formal part of each and every international trade and domestic purchase.

This, the first in a series of International Accords, begins with and is specific to the alignment between

The People's Republic of China and with Canada and its First Nations within.

We hereby acknowledge that China presents a huge appetite for natural resources, and that Canada has abundant resources to offer.

Each and every country shall appoint and maintain an official Grand Ambassador, with the primary purpose of formally setting forth the agreed upon guidelines that thoroughly represent the sanctity of our Earth, all peoples, plants, animals and resources.

- *Whereas, this document, by separate addendum, shall outline in full detail, resource quantities and designations of safe, renewable parameters of consumption for each country.*
- *Whereas each country shall also set forth their respective, projected needs of resources, establishing one worldwide scale from which to satisfy all needs.*

Signed by the above four respective representatives.

The DRAFT sets forth a potential avenue that we could take to protect our resources. If ever there were to be a true Environmental Movement, it will come naturally, from the essence of our always present Loving Universal Consciousness. This pure powerful collective is a massive cleansing action for all of us and for all of the rivers, oceans, lakes, wetlands, jungles, and tundra! The time is NOW to behold our Holy essence and Presence and embrace our natural guided leadership!

There are so many avenues we can take, but first we should establish the gatherings. Please see the exciting video about establishing gatherings at alloneera.com/gatherings. We lovingly invite you to join us!

Please contact me directly to discuss opening a venue - stephen@alloneera.com.

The Summerhill 80 acre Organic Vineyard

"The greatest service
is to show humanity
their divinity."

A clear Guidance received by
Stephen while RAA-gazing (sun-gazing).

Chapter Ten

LOVE STREAM OF CONSCIOUSNESS

As the sweat ran down my forehead while jogging on a crisp early morning in October 2014, a profound message came clearly to me. There was an unmistakable question: "Stephen, will you do anything for humanity?" I instantly blurted out loud, "YES! ANYTHING!"

Slowing my run to a fast walk, I headed toward the beach to find a secluded cluster of woods to continue the dialog. As I sat up on a rock and caught my breath, the communication came back strongly and with a shocking delivery. "You are to go down into the depths of the darkest worlds...into the Netherworld, to be with souls who 'sleep in the dust' – those who have eluded that they are less than grand ambassadors for Holy pure love; those who insist that they have 'fallen from grace,' who believe they are inferior or are not worthy, or who feel consumed by guilt; and those who have resolved that they are 'dead' and do not wish to wake up and join the loving consciousness of the world." I immediately responded that I am a servant above all else and would do anything for humanity; but in my heart of hearts, I began to feel a pang of fear and unpreparedness for such a monumental task.

Within a matter of days, I was on a flight to Japan with Rie and Esther, to spend five weeks with friends and family. During the visit, I lived contrary to my organic vegetarian diet, feasting on exotic Japanese deep-fried tempura and eating fish and I began to have chest pains when I walked fast or exerted myself.

Mid-way through our adventure in Japan, I boarded a plane for China to meet my winery associate, Li Zhou, VP Export. Li and I rendezvoused at a sister organic winery, deep in the wilderness of North China. We were following a plan to spend a week establishing direct marketing of our organic wines and ice wines throughout Asia. After participating in a three day seminar at the winery televised to millions of viewers, and indulging in countless banquet dinners, we took a flight to Shanghai. Upon arrival, our taxi sped its way through horrendous traffic, coming within inches of touching other cars, while topping a speed of over seventy-five miles an hour. While I am a fast driver myself, this ride took my breath away; I had to curl up in the back seat and focus on my breathing to relax. As we wound our way into the heart of Shanghai, I was aghast to be in the heart of a nest of some of the tallest buildings on the planet! Just looking up at the clusters of hundred-plus-story buildings made me dizzy. At street level, there were thousands of people looking so serious, talking or texting on their cell phones, or barking loudly at each other. It shocked me. I was overwhelmed to be in what felt like "hell on earth." I could feel an ache building in my fast beating heart. Perhaps this was an introduction to "The Netherworld," that I was guided to visit, but also maybe there are millions of souls who also sleep in the dust in bodies!

I felt way too uneasy and filled with fear to stay on the 30th floor of the hotel where we had reservations, I immediately opted to switch to a ground floor unit outside of the city in a peaceful park. I was then able to settle down and write notes that took me to echelons of my imagination, never before touched upon. I needed to totally explore the profound Guidance I had received on my lake jog. I came to the realization that indeed the Guidance could only come from what I termed The Celestial Council. A Holy echelon of the entire Loving Universal Consciousness.

I welcomed The Celestial Council, a "buzzing with energy" center of all of life and all of consciousness. I saw that it is made up of ever-revolving and ever-evolving entities that were perhaps in many places at the same time! The Council, as I saw it, was there for everyone at any stage of their lives. It was to show that our lives, all lives, are somehow a part of The Council. It was then that I began to actually see the Light of the council itself! The Light became so bright it was blinding, pulsing and dancing with me and inviting me in! I dove in! I immediately felt so at home. The complete absence of time, space, fear and all emotions was incredible. I was just BEING and just loving BEING!

As an analogy showcasing this vision, we could say that in The Celestial Council *we become* what the First Nations Peoples have honored for eons as *"The Grandfathers and the Grandmothers"* (who can be of any chronological age when they passed, and who speak to us through the sacred fire). In the no time, in multi dimensions and in oneness with all there is, we tap into our Genius-level Knowingness and make our contribution to the evolvement of the whole. This is what occurs when we enter into The Celestial Council – it brings us closest to the actual experience of being one with the whole, simultaneously at all times in our times. The good news is that it's easy! We surrender, allow, allow, allow and open our feminine receiving, and we are welcomed with so much love! We are not on one side or the other, we are one soul in two worlds simultaneously connected – the physical body side and the ethereal body side all at once!

While I was so blessed to have felt The Celestial Council with such peace and clarity during my trip, I began to also feel very strained and stressed. I had been working too hard and eating too many rich foods and not sleeping enough. My blood pressure was mounting and the pains in my chest were coming more and more frequently. Just two days after our return from our trip to Japan and China I suffered a severe life threatening heart attack. Thanks to the Dr. Esselstyn Heart Disease, Cancer and Diabetes Reversal Diet and two stents and plenty of rest, I am happy to say I am now exercising daily and enjoying ultimate health and vitality!

~

May 24, 2015 was Pentecostal Day and serendipitously the anniversary of Moses' ascension of Mount Sinai. On that day, I had an urgent calling to be with The Celestial Council and I called upon angels Metatron and Solé to escort me[43].

---

[43] See alloneera.com/metatronandsole for August 29, 2017 Recording

The Angel Metatron had been in my deepest meditations for all my life. Somehow, his presence had always been felt, but it wasn't until a profound circumstance in the middle of the night more than fifteen years ago, when during a deep meditation, his name was auto-chanted by me, causing me to have a huge jolt. As I blurted his name out loud with astonishment, I had to write it down and research who Metatron was[44]. He has been with me strongly ever since, and I have always been fascinated with this Angel's beguiling energy and circuitous intriguing nature.

On this auspicious Pentecostal day, they Guided me into the Netherworld! Angels Metatron and Solé instilled in me that I had in fact already "completed" my journey. It was already written in the book of life. I instinctively invoked the Knowingness of the Pharaohs, the "I Am," our oneness with RAA and all there is. My Angels escorted me to the "Holy of Holies" – <u>The Celestial Council! The Celestial Council</u> welcomed me. They specifically Guided me to the great work of Moses. I was instantly set on a new, clearer path. It was then that I also more fully understood why, just after returning from the Japan and China trip, I had suffered the heart attack. Metatron instilled, "The death of your heart was not from this life. You had to die again to undo the death that once was."

Being escorted to the purity of the Council grandly aided me in fulfilling my assignment to touch those in the Netherworld, both on this side to those sleeping in bodies and in the ethereal plains.

"By taking away the words, it will unmask the soul within it."
Metatron

The Council honored me by surrounding me in their glorious Holy light and encouraging me to continually radiate their light and these messages, as a conduit and as a businessman. There are indeed so many who are "sleeping in the dust" in bodies. I began looking around and realizing that there are so many to be brought to life here, I began to realize that it is so easy to bring out our awakening to many millions, perhaps billions, of souls! We can all begin to realize how easy it is to leap into and become one with our glorious ever-expanding, ever-loving universe, our splendid creation!

---

[44] Learn more through the Kartron Experience Broadcast at alloneera.com/kartronexperience

The Celestial Council gives us perpetual Guidance to now help to invite all of humanity to ascend and know that indeed we are all one Divine Beings. We all feel privileged and honored to participate in fulfilling this prophecy, the grandest of all of our purpose. I am just another guy on the bus, just another hardworking person who is in service to the whole in any and every way possible. I am reminded of Master Jesus' teaching, "Forgive them. They know not what they do." This wisdom comes alive daily as we rise to having patience with ourselves and with each other. Patience is the core of our collective Selves. All of our experiences enrich the whole, and we are all each other's teachers. We are learning about our Selves by our experiences in bodies, and **we are always totally forgiven**. In fact, loving forgiveness, fortitude and patience ARE our service to the whole! My dad used to always say, "Patience and Fortitude." The great sleeping prophet Edgar Cayce declared **"Time, space and patience are the trinity of Creation."** Patience is a great blessing. Patience with ourselves and patience with others allows us to BE all that we ARE: indeed grand, loving, forgiving, ever-evolving Divine Beings.

On the super-moon of November, 2016, I received another pivotally clear message that speaks to us all: **There is no right or wrong, there is only ONE, one <u>Celestial Council</u> for all there is. We are all conduits of <u>The Celestial Council</u>. They urge us to, "go about your folly, you are Guided, we are with you! Have solace, be confident. You are all greatly loved!"**

When the time comes, we will realize we are all One and every knee shall bend. We each have the magnificent unlimited power within us to affect our entire creation. We ARE God. We ARE Love. Everyone in their heart of hearts knows this most powerful of all universal truths. It is foolish for us to bow down to a separate, fear-based illusion or to "sleep in the dust," when neither is us. In truth, our biggest fear is that of our own Grandness! We have need to take back our power and be who we really are: Grand Beings, co-creating as One. That is when the fear dissipates and our magnificence shines.

There are so many ways to become one with all there is…a "Realized Being." Godance is within us all. This book outlines the return to nature through gatherings and is perhaps a primary place to start. There are no single paths that will play out for everyone. Use your judgement and most of all feel your personal Guidance. Realizing our loving unlimited splendid Selves is the essence of ascension.

> *"We change the world not by what we say or do, but as a consequence of what we have become. Thus, every spiritual aspirant serves the world."*
> Dr. David R. Hawkins

Thank you, Dr. Hawkins, for this grand truth of beholding our Presence, our real gift to the whole. The very essence of the new era that we are so privileged to be in now, is that we can all soar in consciousness, and nourish and expand it exponentially. By returning to our roots as tribal beings through the All One Era gatherings, we honor nature by being one with her. Honoring her moon cycles and season cycles, and being in each other's bands of energy, we merge our all-powerful consciousness! Simply said by my seven year old daughter – "Mother Nature is the real boss of the family, daddy."

Everyone, of all religions and governments, can easily support highest intentions of planet-wide ascension. After all, who doesn't feel the need to be reunited with Mother Nature and her wondrous heartbeat? Who doesn't realize how living in cities has separated us and removed us from being in touch with the heartbeat of nature?

We no longer need to impress anyone; just the opposite. As ascended, loving humans, we will naturally continue to support our robust economies as a vital avenue to ensure a bright future for humanity AND for all of nature. This glorious new era invites a flourishing collective growth through international synergies. Whole nations will eventually relax their borders and merge together! Religions will continue to exist, but maybe not in their present format. Perhaps by emphasizing each of their respective lofty roots, and focusing on their similarities, rather than their differences, they will flourish. Together we will all know that the most powerful prayer is for our perpetual health, prosperity and joy to flourish. I coin this prayer by a mighty declaration at the beginning of each day. I lift my full glass of water and say aloud, "To Life! For <u>EVER</u> and <u>EVER</u>

and <u>EVER</u>! So be it and so it is!" While reverence for the Grand Teachings is vital, giving away our power to any entity or religion detracts from our triumph in merging with the Loving Universal Consciousness. We are blessed with having the foundation from which we can soar together to ever grander loving consciousness, with no limitations and no separation. The basic realization of the Golden Rule, which is the foundation of all religions, **do unto others as you would have them do unto you,** is also the golden thread that ties us all together.

Quantum physics demonstrates conclusively how affecting global change is in our hands! It is WE who determine our future. It is WE who are now taking back our power and clarifying our original sublime intention and purpose. This new (to us) science clearly shows how we manifest our reality from moment-to-moment. Now we are realizing that *there are none greater than we.* As participants in Guidance, we merge with all beings, and all life, we ascend in our true Grandness. It is WE who through our very blessed and powerful intentional gatherings, return our Selves and our world to its natural loving joyous thriving wellness.

As my dad used to say, "If you don't enjoy yourself, who will?"

May we be renewed and each of us be blessed in our eternal, sublime Purpose. May we revel on this, our splendid blue-green spinning playground. May we rejuvenate Her and our Selves to ultimate health, vigor, abundance, joy, and ever-expanding consciousness! May we take action and BE the ones we've been waiting for. Selah!

Respectfully, lovingly and gratefully submitted,
Stephen Cipes

My Circa 1975 Vanity License Plate in New York, now on the '51 Ford 1 Ton on the vineyard.

"The tragedy of life
is what dies inside a man
while he lives."

Albert Einstein

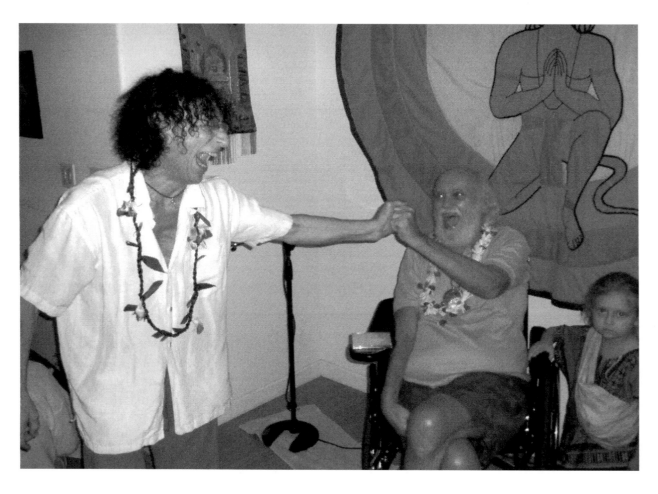

Stephen and Ram Dass (aka Dr. Richard Alpert), in Hawaii. Ram Dass is the author of
Be Here Now, a 1971 phenomenon book with millions of copies sold.

I AM that which IS.

This Holy sentiment was magically captured by "The Way Out" in the 2002 recording, Get Out of Your Head. Get Into Your Heart.[45]

---

[45] See alloneera.com/getoutofyourhead for the full lyrics

GLOSSARY OF TERMS

The All One Era –

The prophesized era of our return to our Holy state of oneness with all there is that officially began at the end of the ancient Mayan lunar calendar on December 21, 2012. As ascended humans, our oneness with all there is, is fully realized; as an ascended humanity, our Original Splendid Intention of love and of knowing our Selves is renewed and flourishes. The key to our ascension is Knowingness; the key to Knowingness is surrender; the key to surrender is relaxing our ego and welcoming our feminine receiving; the key to receiving is allowing spirit to flow through us as conduits, as microcosms of the universe; the key to becoming a conduit is proactively loving life and all there is.

The All One Era is our unified conscious alignment. It is a period known as the Age of Aquarius, or the Messianic Age, or the Christ Consciousness Age. This is a time of mergence with the Holy loving energy that we eternally are.

All One Era Prophecy –

The prophecy of the All One Era is that we know in our heart of hearts that we are God, the original creators of the universe, all-Knowing and all one. This revelation is undeniable, because this is who we are. There is no separation between us and the creation of matter which is the slowed vibration of our energy. Energy is love, the glue of the universe, a want to love ourselves and all there is…better known as Oneness. This is a circular perspective.

The essence of this "prophecy of prophecies" lies deep in all of our soul memories.

The Celestial Council –

The Celestial Council is also known as "The Holy of Holies". It is an always "buzzing with energy" center of all of life's consciousness. It is made up of ever-revolving and ever-evolving entities! The council, as I saw it, was there for everyone at any stage of their lives. It is to show that our lives, all lives, are (through LUC) part of the council. The complete absence of all thought, time, space, fear and all emotions, a stillness. In the no time in multi dimensions and in oneness with all there is, we enter into our Genius-level Knowingness and are privileged to make our contribution to the evolvement of the whole. We become closest to actually being one with the whole, simultaneously and at all times.

Conduits of Spirit –

We become Conduits of Spirit when we open our Feminine Receiving Selves (X chromosomes) to Guidance. It is a very subtle occurrence; you often don't know it until after it happens. As Conduits, our bodies become our microcosms of the universe, our tools to create; and we, as the collective Holy creators, become one with all there is! It is from this "seat of the soul" that we became instruments of pure spirit, pure consciousness, pure creative essence, filled with love for all there is.

Divine –

The Enchanted, all-knowing, mysterious, wispy, fairy-like Holy Presence. Often referred to as God, Allah, Christ or Buddha or the unspeakable. The essence of the life itself, the vibration of Light, that we are.

Feminine Receiving Selves –

Men have one X and one Y Chromosome. Women have two X Chromosomes. The Y is the male aggression trait and the X is the female receiving loving trait. It is easier for females to be receivers of LUC but we men can do it! The practice of releasing/surrendering our natural ego that all of us in Goded bodies have. Living in a state of receivership opens us into multi-dimensional Guidance as conduits of Divine Spirit.

Forever Beings / Forever Selves –

We are our soul memories of all our incarnations going back eons. There is no beginning, there is no end; there is no time per se, there is only the now. We are all one forever beings, no separation, ever evolving Holy creators.

Genius-Level (Selves/Knowingness) –

Within us all we hold genius, the unlimited knowingness of our Grand Creation in all of its glorious dimensions. There is no darkness, there is only light. There is no separation, we share each other's trials and tribulations, sicknesses, pain, suffering and triumphs. There are none in all the universe who know more than we do, we are genius grand forever beings indeed!

God Love –

The words "God" and "Love" are synonymous, because you can't have one without the other. God is the glory of our nature, and love upholds that.

Grand Selves –

The Master within us. We all have a genius-level knowingness that we own, that is a part of us. While subliminal, it is all there, part of our DNA. We ALL have this.

Grand Teachings –

These are the teachings of the Realized Beings that have come forth in our recent history (the last 10,000 years) – Krishna, Moses, Jesus and the thousands of others who are with us today, and have always been with us, who fully understand and love who we are. Many of the Grand Teachings are eloquently set forth, though some have been sadly distorted to allow fear to reign. The Grand Teachings are and have always been all around us, though many of them have been subdued, because it was felt that we were not ready for them. In the All One Era, we are ready and they are freely flowing now. In fact, we are each becoming Realized Beings and sharing our insights and wisdoms as never before.

Guidance AKA Godance –

Our revelation that we are all Guided and an integral part of the LUC versus us egotistically gloating over our individual achievements or being disappointed in our failures. It is found in subtle Knowingness that is sometimes seen only in later reflection.

Godance is acknowledging Guidance for our Divine Selves.

Holy (with a capital "H") –

The living Light of the essence of all life and all there is. A reverence from our Selves resounding our complete recognition of the vibrations of greatest possible magnitude.

Knowingness (with a capital "K") –

That magical, wispy, silent yet loud, transparent yet color-filled feeling of joy that titillates every atom of every cell in our bodies. It is a word that has no element of doubt and aptly describes our ability to be conduits of the cosmic and natural vibrations that surround each of us and all there is at all times. Such a vibration can be enhanced greatly as we align our lives with love, gratitude and a return to an organic nature.

Knowingness (or Consciousness) can be thought of as "The Void," because there is the absence of matter. In a state of Knowingness, whether it is for a fleeting moment or at all times, it is like floating between where the stars and their planets revolve, or between where the neutrons and protons of atoms revolve. It is the resting place where our universe is created. It is the place from which we manifest matter. This void or empty space is the cosmic glue that unites us all.

Loving Universal Consciousness (LUC) –

The sea of consciousness we all contribute to and take from. It is our collection of greatest vibration and Holy loving energy that is always present. When we go within to our hearts, our soul memories, our essence, and our Knowingness, we connect with what I call the ever-present Loving Universal Consciousness, the LUC; you can call it intuition, consciousness, or anything that feels right.

Microcosm of the Macrocosm –

Each human being has all of the components of the entire universe. We, individually with our miraculous electrical in nature bodies, are a physical microcosm of the entire macrocosm, the whole of the universe. Each cell is made of atoms, which in themselves have proportions of the void to matter of the entire universe (see Nassim Haramein).

Oneness –

The empathy, understanding, cherishing, contemplation, compassion, forgiveness and unconditional love for ourselves, revealing us to be one with all there are and all there is.

Original Splendid Intentions –

Our Original Splendid Intention that sprang from "the VOID" when we realized our <u>Self</u> (the BIG BANG THEORY). We immediately began to create a physical universe based on our revelation of love of Self! It is our setting forth an ever-expanding Loving Universal Consciousness, both physical and spiritual. We are all from one original entity. We are naturally one with ascension consciousness. It is the exuberance of life itself – the little boy, little girl exuberance for life that makes us tingle with joy. Our Original Splendid Intention is to feel our oneness with all there is, and to allow it to reverberate through our lives, as we lovingly and patiently express it.

Realized Being –

A Realized Being is a "God/Goddess" in a body…one who is one with all there is and who proactively acknowledges, receives and is one with the Holy loving energies that surround us as we co-create our universe from moment to moment.

ABOUT THE AUTHOR

Stephen Cipes is "Uncle Steve" to an entourage of kids…after all, he IS a kid! "I never like to be serious. Life is fun…this is our playground!" Stephen likes to run along the lake at daybreak every day and greet the sun. He loves playing with his little daughter and all of his grandchildren every chance he gets.

He is busy (busy hands are happy hands) making extraordinary organic wines. He has envisioned a model of "man and nature" and a venue for the "Grand teachings" on the magnificent 80-acre organic vineyard and nature preserve in Kelowna, British Columbia. He has built a four-story, fused-frame pyramid as close to the absolute precision and alignment of The Great Pyramid of Egypt as possible with today's technology (the ancient civilization had technology we don't (yet) have today). In 1997 he established gatherings in the pyramid and around the sacred fire in the Kekuli, welcoming the community to full and new moon Solstice and Equinox gatherings. The daily "Pyramid Experience" tours attract thousands of visitors a day.

Stephen's foresight, initiative and passion for organics and the unity of humanity have earned him international acclaim. In 2003, he received the prestigious Ernst and Young *Entrepreneur of the Year Award* in the hospitality category. In 2004, he was named *A Friend of the United Nations*, alongside Yoko Ono and His Holiness, The Dalai Lama, for his work with Indigo Children. In 2016, he was given *The Founder's Award* for his contribution to the British Columbia wine industry.

While actively involved in the day-to-day activities at Summerhill, Stephen's bursting energy takes him running daily with the vigor of a young boy. He shares his profound spiritual nature with children of all ages, and enjoys his four sons and four daughters-in-law, six grandchildren, and wife Rie (pronounced Ria) and little daughter Esther, the apple of his eye! He welcomes emails and personal calls at stephen@alloneera.com and 1-833-ALL-1-ERA.

Stephen pouring Cipes Brut on the 30th Anniversary of the
Summerhill Organic Winery October 11, 2016.
summerhillpyramid.com
alloneera.com
stephencipes.com
1-833-ALL-1-ERA

86046583R00107

Made in the USA
Columbia, SC
24 December 2017